ANIMAL EXTINCTIONS

What Everyone Should Know

ANIMAL EXTINCTIONS

What Everyone Should Know

EDITED
by R.J.HOAGE

Smithsonian Institution Press   Washington, D.C.   London

Library of Congress Cataloging in Publication Data
Main entry under title:
Animal extinctions

  (National Zoological Park symposia for the
public series)
    1. Extinct animals.   2. Extinction (Biology)
I. Hoage, R. J.   II. Series.
QL88.A55   1985   333.95'416   85-8342
ISBN 0-87474-521-7

**National Zoological Park Symposia for
the Public**

This series brings before the public a variety
of intriguing and controversial issues in wildlife biology and conservation. Complicated topics are addressed. Problems are analyzed. In
many cases, solutions are provided and discussed. The goal of these books is to provide
information to stimulate public awareness
and discussion of the problems that animals
and their habitats face in a world increasingly
dominated by human beings.

To: Ada,
Alden,
and Patti

The 12 chapters in this volume are derived from oral presentations given at the first National Zoological Park Symposium for the Public, September 11 and 12, 1982.

Contents

12

Cultural Loss Can Foreshadow Human Extinctions: The Influence of Modern Civilization

COLIN M. TURNBULL

List of Contributors

David Challinor
Assistant Secretary for Science
Smithsonian Institution
Washington, D.C. 20560

Paul R. Ehrlich
Bing Professor of Population Studies
Department of Biological Sciences
Stanford University
Stanford, California 94305

Robert J. Hoage
Special Assistant to the Director
National Zoological Park
Smithsonian Institution
Washingtion, D.C. 20008

Stephen R. Humphrey
Associate Curator of Ecology
Florida State Museum
Gainesville, Florida 32611

Robert E. Jenkins
Vice President
Director of Science Programs
The Nature Conservancy
1800 North Kent Street
Arlington, Virginia 22209

Thomas E. Lovejoy
Vice President for Science
World Wildlife Fund-USA
1601 Connecticut Avenue, N.W.
Washington, D.C. 20009

Eugene S. Morton
Research Zoologist
Department of Zoological Research
National Zoological Park
Smithsonian Institution
Washington, D.C. 20008

Norman Myers
Consultant in Environment and Development
Upper Meadow, Old Road
Headington, Oxford, Great Britain

Elliott A. Norse
Public Policy Director
The Ecological Society of America
1601 Connecticut Avenue, N.W.
Washington, D.C. 20009

Theodore H. Reed
Director (1958–1983)
National Zoological Park
Smithsonian Institution
Washington, D.C. 20008

Ulysses S. Seal
Veterans Administration Medical Center
Building 49, Room 207
54th Street & 48th Avenue S.
Minneapolis, Minnesota 55417

Steven M. Stanley
Professor of Paleobiology
Department of Earth and Planetary Sciences

Johns Hopkins University
Baltimore, Maryland 21218

Colin M. Turnbull
Professor of Anthropology
Department of Anthropology
George Washington University
2112 G Street, N.W.
Washington, D.C. 22503

Preface

Picture a herd of warm weather-loving, duck-billed dinosaurs browsing peacefully beside a pond in a Florida reserve, perhaps even in a five-acre paddock at the new, expansive Metropolitan Miami Zoo. What an image! What a bonanza this would be for science, the arts, and the satisfaction of human curiosity! At least for one dinosaur species we would no longer have to guess about its behavior, skin color and texture, smell, locomotion, sounds, and reproduction.

Because we do not yet know if mankind can save elephants or rhinoceroses for the next 100 or 500 years, it is reasonable to wonder whether humans, if they had evolved 80-million years earlier, could have developed wildlife preservation techniques soon enough to have saved even one small population of dinosaurs so that we could see and experience them today.

If we are not successful in preserving today's great pachyderms our descendants, of course, will still be able to see them. Like the tyrannosaurs, brontosaurs, stegosaurs, triceratops, and other dinosaurs, elephants, rhinoceroses, giraffes, and hippopotamuses will make excellent displays in museums—stuffed, shellacked, and painted, with no smells, no sounds, no motion, and no life behind their eyes.

There are those who might say that preserving small populations of animals in captivity and in reserves is artificial preservation—that it is not natural to adapt animals to human management. In this view, the "wildness" of a species would diminish over time when its natural habitat, its niche, had been made to conform to human demands. Other critics might say that humans are "playing God" by selecting certain species and habitats for preservation, thus permitting other extinctions to occur. These people may feel that it is more natural to let animals become extinct than to come under human management. But, in my mind, the image of that herd of duck-billed dinosaurs being maintained in a zoo, despite their survival under human sponsorship, clearly outweighs their permanent loss.

Humanity is only now beginning to attempt to master the long-term preservation of animals in captivity and in game preserves and national parks—the last refuges for an increasing number of species. The success of these efforts, in truth, will not be known for several centuries. Much needs to be done in our lifetimes and our children's lifetimes to ensure that even a small number of these efforts will be successful.

At present, thinking in terms of a time span longer than one's lifetime seems to be difficult for many people. A kind of generational ego-centrism, which accepts short-term, quick fix solutions to environmental problems, seems to exist in many human populations. A major question is whether the solutions for today's problems will solve the problems for tomorrow's generations. The idea of creating and establishing a 500-year conservation plan, especially one concerned with the preservation of species and habitats, is revolutionary.

Yet even if nothing is done evolution will continue—albeit not in a manner we might think of as normal. Species that can or already have adapted to human culture and technology will very likely survive. Good candidates for this kind of survival include cockroaches, rats, mice, house sparrows, starlings, pigeons, squirrels, raccoons, and bats, among others. Domesticated animals could also be included in this category. However, it remains to be seen if the "human niche" can continue to be exploited by these animals in the millenia to come.

The concept of extinction—what it means today and has meant in the past—was at the heart of the first National Zoological Park symposium for the public. The symposium was developed to bring before the public the important issues that surround the elimination of species and habitats. It is clear that these issues are complex, not easy to comprehend in many cases, and give rise to differing opinions. The topics covered at the symposium were designed to acquaint the interested public with a variety of scientific approaches to critical problems and possible solutions. I think the presentations in this volume will be a useful source of public information that will help foster discussion and understanding of the controversy among those who view every extinction as a biological disaster, those who accept extinction as a normal process in evolution, and those who are alarmed primarily by the accelerating rate of human-induced extinctions. The latter group sees these current extinctions as different from past ones and views the elimination of species today not just as the loss of individual competing species within ecological communities but as a foreshadowing of the disruption and loss of widespread, complex habitats—habitats that provide essential ecological goods and services such as clean air and water, productive soils, and many still unidentified harvestable products. Many of the participants in this symposium are in this camp, and their objections to allowing the ever-increasing rate of modern extinctions are compelling. Anyone exposed to the information they present must realize that major decisions must soon be made regarding the prevention or acceptance of modern extinctions.

It is important to remember that decisions will have to be made by persons who have the knowledge to make intelligent choices. People need to know what the issues and problems are, what solutions may or may not yet exist, and what the consequences may be if decisions are not made. This is what the symposium was all about—bringing information about a complex wildlife problem, a global problem, to the public in a fashion that can be easily understood.

There are those who ask why a zoo is an appropriate location to have such a gathering; after all, zoos are primarily facilities for recreation and entertainment, not places where serious scientific discussions occur. People who understand the functions of a modern zoo know that the contrary is true. More and more, large zoos are becoming involved in major scientific research projects to better understand how species can be propagated and maintained in captivity. While remaining centers of recreation, zoos have become places where significant scientific work takes place. Educating the public about animal behavior, biology, and ecology has become an important objective.

The 12 papers in this volume are derived from oral presentations recorded during the symposium. They can be grouped into three categories: those that define specific problems and present methods for preserving species or habitats (Humphrey, Seal, and Jenkins); those that are scientific essays focusing on both specific and general aspects of the extinction phenomenon (Challinor, Stanley, Lovejoy, Morton, and Turnbull); and those that explore the global implications of species' extinction, using numerous examples of human involvement in the elimination of animals and plants

(Norse, Ehrlich, and Myers). All of them are presented in a lively style, still charged with the enthusiasm of their original presentation.

What is most exciting and unusual about this symposium is that, although I, as editor of this volume, have read and reread drafts of each paper several times, I am as enthusiastic as ever about the topics addressed. I hope that those who read these papers will be similarly stimulated with just one exposure.

Acknowledgments: Financial support received from the Continental Group Foundation, the Friends of the National Zoo, and a third organization that prefers to remain anonymous made the symposium possible. Former director of the National Zoo, Dr. Theodore H. Reed, and former assistant director for Animal Programs, Dr. John F. Eisenberg, provided advice and support. The staff and volunteers of the National Zoo's Office of Public Affairs, Michael Morgan, Ilene Ackerman, and Sharon Pailen, were unfailing in their efforts to assist in this undertaking, as was Rodney Brown, the Friends of the National Zoo audiovisual equipment operator. Rod Brown's technical know-how made each presentation a pleasure to see and hear.

I am especially grateful to Nancy O'Rourke, volunteer to the Friends of the National Zoo, for her dedicated efforts to initiate the production of these proceedings. Almost single-handedly, she took the transcripts of the speakers' presentations, edited and rewrote substantial parts of each one, and skillfully worked the revised speakers' comments into the manuscripts. Ms. O'Rourke is largely responsible for converting the oral presentations, nearly incomprehensible in written form, into highly readable manuscripts that could be returned to the authors for first and second reviews. Without her year-long persistence at this task, the symposium proceedings would today be only half complete. Ms. O'Rourke deserves special recognition for her work.

Dr. Nancy Muckenhirn, National Zoo research associate, critiqued several of the later manuscript drafts for scientific accuracy. She cheerfully edited and rewrote certain difficult sections that would have proved taxing to even the most incisive mind. Dr. Muckenhirn also researched incomplete citations and found several illustrations that were used as models for figures. Her efforts have helped to make this volume both readable and easy to understand.

Artists Sally Bensusen, Kathleen Spagnola, Vichai Malikul, and Sigrid Bruch contributed figures. Their illustrations provide visual highlights to many of the papers.

Tabetha Carpenter of the National Zoo was exceptional in her willingness to use both typewriter and word processor to produce numerous manuscript drafts. Ms. Carpenter exhibited a dedication and fondness for this project that inspired the rest of us working on it to persevere even during the most frustrating moments.

Finally, I must thank my wife Patti, who helped to make this work possible. Her enthusiastic interest in and support of these undertakings were invaluable.

R. J. HOAGE

Welcome Address

THEODORE H. REED

These past 24 years, during which I have been director of the National Zoological Park, have been extremely interesting for all of us working here. We have seen many changes not only here in Washington, with much construction and development at the zoo, but also in the overall public interest and sense of responsibility that have accompanied an increased awareness and concern for the other animals with which we share this planet. There is today a deeper realization that we are one of many species in the animal kingdom—a special one it is true, but one that is more keenly aware that the fate of our fellow animals on this earth will ultimately affect and, to a large extent, depend on us.

When I first became associated with zoos 35 years ago, the plains of Africa seemed to have unlimited numbers of animals. In those days, there was little general concern about conservation. Thinking people and professionals in the field were concerned but not the general public. There was not the widespread interest, such as we see now, in what is happening in the Amazon Basin, in Southeast Asia, and in other parts of the world. When I first came here, I could buy animals from dealers who would phone me up and say, "Hey, Ted, I got a shipment of animals. What do you want?" We would dicker back and forth, and I would decide what I would take, or I would go to see the shipment of animals myself. If I wanted an animal, I would place an order, and lo and behold it would appear. Now we have numerous good and sound protective laws for animals. We work through the game departments of foreign lands. It sometimes takes as long as six or seven months just to get permits to export or to import certain animals. We must justify the particular imports we propose by describing our programs. A complete change has occurred during these years in the way that we in the zoos look at animals and the way the public looks at them. Visitors used to just enjoy the animals, seeing them as cute or strange, lovable or scary. Now visitors are coming and asking what zoos are doing about trying to preserve animals on the verge of extinction.

Today the National Zoological Park is doing a considerable amount of work in preservation and conservation. We are involved in many cooperative animal-breeding programs with other zoos. We have our own breeding farm at Front Royal, Virginia, where we have a number of rather large herds of exotic and endangered animals. Our herd of Père David's deer, a species extinct in the wild, is the largest in the United States. The National Zoo has made a long-term commitment to maintain this captive population. I hope that future directors of this zoo will continue the programs we have begun. If this happens, we will have Père David's deer, European bison, lion tamarin monkeys, and several other species of animals maintained for future generations of American children. Our grandchildren and our great-grandchildren may still be able to see these animals because of what we are doing now. Thirty years ago, people used to feel that zoos might be the last refuge for Przewalskis horses, Père David's deer, Nene geese, and perhaps one or two other species. But there has recently been an interesting change in philosophy. Now people are saying that zoos will be the only hope for dozens of endangered animals.

In addition to becoming involved in captive husbandry, zoos are becoming increasingly attentive to conditions in the wild that may contribute to the extinction of many species. This is one of the reasons for this symposium, which brings together a distinguished group of concerned experts from various fields. I am delighted to have this meeting here as one more step toward understanding the causes of extinction and what we may be able to do about them.

I

Introductory Address:

What Everyone Should Know About Animal Extinctions

DAVID CHALLINOR

I have been asked this morning to open this symposium. My address is entitled "What Everyone Should Know About Animal Extinctions." The very large number of you participating here is dramatic evidence of the importance of this topic. On behalf of the Smithsonian Institution, of which the National Zoological Park is a part, I welcome you all most warmly.

Let us review our topic. First, while all living organisms are subject to extinction, in this symposium we will be concerned basically with animals—including people. Second, according to the dictionary, when something is extinct it no longer exists; it has been eliminated or extinguished. What concerns us today is the *process* of extinction, which is generally very intricate. The reasons for animal extinction are many and complicated.

Since mammals first appeared in the late Triassic Period, about 200-million years ago, more mammal species have arisen and become extinct than live in the world today. Perhaps two-thirds or more of all the animal species that ever existed on this planet are now no more. But if extinction is such a natural and inevitable process, why should we all be so concerned about it today? The reasons should become clear in the course of this symposium.

As the earth's environment changes, plants and animals obviously become vulnerable when they can no longer adapt successfully to those changes. Qualities that often limit adaptation in mammals, for example, are large size and/or a highly specialized diet, both of which are difficult to modify quickly in the evolutionary process—that is, over a few animal generations. Dr. Humphrey will discuss aspects of this phenomenon following my address, and later Dr. Stanley will consider extinction as part of the natural evolutionary process.

The disappearance of vulnerable species can create space in an ecosystem for the evolution of new forms that have the genetic potential to supplant those that have become extinct. For example, mammals have become the dominant form of life on earth, replacing the dinosaurs who reigned supreme for millions of years. Dinosaurs evolved 160-million years ago and were successful for a long time. They have now entirely disappeared, although some feel that the tuatara—a small lizard-like creature living on several small islands off northern New Zealand—may be a surviving distant relative. For all practical purposes, however, the dinosaurs are gone.

The fossil record clearly indicates that extinction is the norm and survival the exception. It also shows that once an animal has disappeared, it does not reappear. The existence of a species is a one-way trip, even though a given species can sometimes endure for a few hundred million years. The ancient survivors are the ones that intrigue us. The horseshoe crab, for example, has been in existence for hundreds of millions of years. In 1938 the coelecanth, an extremely ancient fish, was discovered still surviving in the southwest corner of the Indian Ocean. This fish has remained unchanged since the Carboniferous Period, three- or four-hundred million years ago. The coelecanth evidently found a stable niche in the Comoro Island waters that allowed it to survive during this incredibly long period.

Zoos such as the National Zoological Park can play an important part in slowing extinction rates for some animal species and can sometimes expand endangered populations by captive breeding for ultimate release to the wild. However, the very act of such controlled breeding profoundly alters the selective pressures to which these animals were formerly subjected. Because it is complicated and expensive to breed endangered animals, zoos generally try to raise the maximum number of offspring to maintain the largest possible breeding pool. Thus, it is inevitable that some genetically impaired individuals, that never would have left the nest or the den in wild populations, avoid in captivity many of the pressures of natural selection. We therefore can unwittingly produce new strains in zoo animals that, although outwardly resembling their wild counterparts, probably could not survive long in the wild without direct human intervention. Zoos also maintain small populations of rare animals no longer living in the wild that probably could never be reintroduced to their original habitats. The expense and research necessary to sustain this effort can usually be afforded only by zoos in prosperous nations. Such animal preservation may be justified for the aesthetic pleasure the animals give the beholder. We would like our great-great-grandchildren to be able to see in the flesh some of the elegant animals that in the future will have long disappeared in the wild. In addition, such species may conceivably furnish an unexpectedly valuable product to mankind in the future. This is another reason for keeping them in zoos, even though we are more likely to reap such future benefits from unspoiled ecosystems rather than from the preservation of individual species.

Just as genetic manipulation has long been practiced by the livestock industry to produce qualities considered valuable by breeders, so have zoos used this technique to "recreate" extinct species. For example, beginning in the 1930s programs were begun in Poland and Germany to breed domesticated horses for primitive traits to produce animals that had the external characteristics of the tarpan, a wild European horse that became extinct in the nineteenth century. These "inbred" tarpans can still be seen in several European and American zoos. A fascinating account of this breeding experiment is in Grzimek's *Animal Life Encyclopedia (1974)*. However, although these tarpans resemble their wild ancestors, they are not the same animal. The original is extinct, and because of this it can never be recreated.

Breeding exotic animals in captivity and propagating collections of exotic plants were for centuries hobbies of the rich and powerful. We know, for example, that Chinese emperors kept Père David's deer in their imperial gardens, and much later Great Britain's Duke of Bedford was instrumental in the captive preservation of this deer species. Such activities were probably carried out primarily for amusement or for aesthetic reasons. Nonetheless, time and posterity have validated their importance on much broader grounds with regard to human responsibility for the world we share with other creatures. Today such private activities are virtually impossible, and only large, well-supported public institutions can afford elaborate animal-breeding programs.

Breeding programs, however, are only part of the answer. If reintroductions to the wild are to take place, there must be available habitats in which to relocate these animals. Most contemporary extinctions seem to be attributable to human activity. It is therefore important for us to understand the human effect on the wild biota (plant and animal life of any region). Unwittingly, we may be losing many more species than we realize because we have not had time to identify all the plants and animals, particularly in the tropical rainforests, that are so rapidly being destroyed.

Some of the anticipated consequences of human pressures on animal populations will be discussed this afternoon by Dr. Myers.

Complete preservation of any given ecosystem is neither economically nor politically practical nor even possible, given current human activities. We should, however, keep working on reasonable compromises regarding land use. We must identify the limits within which an ecosystem can safely be manipulated for our short-run needs while still retaining the capacity to protect endangered species and to preserve the existing flora and fauna for potential new sources of food and medicine. While considering specific ecosystems, we must not lose sight of the global one, which could unwittingly be so altered by human activity that its capacity to support human existence becomes strained. We are aware, for example, of some of the effects of acid rain, but the consequences of carbon dioxide imbalance in the atmosphere are less clearly understood. We must never forget that humans, too, are vulnerable to extinction.

The question of what to do about animal extinctions is even more difficult to answer than why we should be concerned in the first place. One approach might be to consider using the "triage system" to govern choices about which animals to save. This would require decisions as to (1) which animals would survive anyway with little or no effort, (2) which might survive with immediate and intensive effort, and (3) which are unlikely to survive even with great effort and therefore must be let alone and allowed to become extinct. Scientists are seeking acceptable premises for making these kinds of decisions. We will be discussing this problem during the course of the symposium. One difficulty can be illustrated by the National Zoological Park's elaborate breeding program of the golden lion tamarin. This golden-furred monkey is unbelievably beautiful but is not the only endangered marmoset. Other marmosets with slightly different coloration may be just as important, but we have picked the golden one primarily for aesthetic reasons. It seems doubtful that humans can make unemotional decisions on what to save. Another important issue is how to invest the available financial resources to combat animal extinctions most effectively, especially in trying to preserve ecosystems that are most threatened by human population growth.

During this symposium, you will hear some imaginative ways to combat both animal extinctions and habitat loss on local and global levels. Dr. Seal will examine problems of preserving animals in captivity; Dr. Norse will discuss the value of animal and plant species for agriculture, industry, and as a source of medicines; and Dr. Myers will describe the current spasm of extinctions and its implications for the future. Tomorrow morning, Drs. Lovejoy, Myers, and Jenkins will discuss various strategies for preserving species in their natural habitats and for conservating those habitats. Tomorrow afternoon, Dr. Morton will consider the problem of reintroducing populations into the wild; Dr. Ehrlich will describe some of the recent grave and dangerous developments that may affect animal extinctions; and Dr. Turnbull will give the symposium's final presentation—an exploration of the concept of extinction in a human cultural setting.

There is no single approach to the problem of animal extinctions, nor are there simple answers. Some speakers' ideas will be controversial. The symposium's goal is to answer some basic questions and to generate information that may clarify some of the confusion surrounding this topic. I hope that everyone in attendance will gain a better appreciation of the enormous complexity of the problem and learn of ways in which we all may be able to cope with it. We need to appreciate the inherent dilemma of choosing what survives and what does not, and what to expect in the future if nothing is done to stem the current tide of disappearing species and habitats. Lastly, I hope these two days will stimulate you to do some investigation and research on your own, to come to your own conclusions, and to lend your support at this critical time.

An informed person, who knows the issues, can take action in a number of ways. Many conservation organizations are worth supporting; some even participate in international projects designed to save wildlife in fast-disappearing habitats. Zoos, museums, and botanical gardens are involved in conservation education, and some of them, like the Smithsonian's National Zoo, have developed their own overseas conservation projects. Most of these kinds of institutions have participatory programs that support conservation activities; they may be just the vehicle through which your energies could be channelled.

Another approach for the concerned citizen is to make his or her views known. Letters—to elected officials on the local, state, and national levels; to radio, TV, and newspaper editors; and to corporate executives and members of boards of directors of corporations—can have an effect. Also, make your views known to friends and other people. Let them know how they can become involved in and support conservation programs.

Finally, we must all be careful about purchasing pets or plants or wild animal products. Many animals and plants are legally protected. You *can* ask a seller to provide documentation to prove that what you are buying is a legal purchase. Such precautions will help make illegal trade that much more difficult.

References Cited and Additional Readings

Barney, G. O., ed.
1980.   The Global 2000 Report to the President—Entering the Twenty-First Century, Vol. I. Washington, D.C.: U.S. Government Printing Office.

Bendiner, R.
1981.   *The Fall of the Wild—The Rise of the Zoo.* New York: E. P. Dutton.

Burton, M. and R. Burton.
1978.   *The World's Disappearing Wildlife.* New York: Arco Publishing.

Cox, J. A.
1975.   *The Endangered Ones.* New York: Crown Publishers.

Day, D.
1981.   *The Doomsday Book of Animals—A Natural History of Vanished Species.* New York: Viking-Penguin.

Eckholm, E.
1978.   *Disappearing Species: The Social Challenge.* Worldwatch Paper, 22 July.

Ehrlich, P. and A. Ehrlich
1981.   *Extinction—The Causes and Consequences of the Disappearance of Species.* New York: Random House.

Ford, B.
1981.   *Alligators, Raccoons and Other Survivors—The Wildlife of the Future.* New York: William Morrow and Co.

Frankel, O. H. and M. E. Soule.
1981.   *Conservation and Evolution.* New York: Cambridge University Press.

Grzimek, B.
1974.   *Grzimek's Animal Life Encyclopedia* (13 vols.). New York and London: Van Nostrand Reinhold Co.

Holliday, T.
1978.   *Vanishing Birds: Their Natural History and Conservation.* New York: Holt, Rinehart and Winston.

Hoose, P. M.
1981.   *Building an Ark: Tools for the Preservation of Natural Diversity Through Land Protection.* Covelo, Calif.: Island Press.

Jenkins, A. C.
1973.   *Wildlife in Danger.* New York: Martin.

A N I M A L

Lovejoy, T.
1976.   We must decide which species will go forever. *Smithsonian* 4: 52–59.

Martin, R. D.
1975.   *Breeding Endangered Species in Captivity.* New York: Academic Press.

Miller, J. A. and D. Franklin.
1981.   Breeding new life into endangered species. *Science News* 120(22): 347–348.

Myers, N.
1980.   The problem of disappearing species: what can be done? *American Biologist*: 229–235.

Myers, N.
1979.   *The Sinking Ark.* Oxford: Pergamon Press.

Norse, E. and R. McManus.
1980.   Biological Diversity. *The Eleventh Annual Report of the Council on Environmental Quality.* December: 1–49.

Reiss, S.
1980.   Vanishing forests. *Newsweek*, November 24, 117–22.

Soule, M. E. and B. A. Wilcox
1980.   *Conservation Biology—An Evolutionary-Ecological Perspective.* Sunderland, Mass.: Sinauer Associates.

Stanley, S. M.
1981.   *The New Evolutionary Timetable.* New York: Basic Books.

Ullrich, W.
1971.   *Endangered Species.* New York: Hart Publishing Co.

Ziswiler, V.
1965.   *Extinct and Vanishing Animals.* London: The English Universities Press.

2

How Species Become Vulnerable To Extinction
And How We Can Meet The Crises

STEPHEN R. HUMPHREY

Though perhaps surprising, I would liken concern with extinction to a very serious love affair. Like love, concern about endangered species is a risky imperative. I once saw a tree on a subtropical Florida Key on which two tourists had sentimentally carved their names, Jerry and Ana, complete with a traditional heart pierced with Cupid's arrow. In a maladroit expression of their great joy at seeing the unfamiliar forest about them, Jerry and Ana chose a poisonwood tree (*Metopium toxiferum*) as a tablet (Figure 1). What they did not know was that this lovely tree trunk contains alkaloids, the same chemicals that repel North Americans from poison ivy. Their expression of love probably proved irritating to the fingers.

The point is that to love well, we must love carefully—we must know what we are doing. To consider what we can do for endangered species is the objective of this symposium. All of us here are indeed in love with the natural world or we would not be at this gathering. Yet knowing what action to take is also a problem. So let us review some of the biological processes and management practices that are involved when species become vulnerable to extinction.

ADAPTATIONS AND VULNERABILITY

Species vulnerable to extinction can be categorized into three types, two of which are inherently vulnerable because of their biological predisposition

Figure I   *Poisonwood tree (Metopium toxiferum) with initials carved on it. Illustration by Kathleen Spagnola.*

to becoming extinct. For these two types, we have the advantage of being able to predict events from our biological knowledge. Therefore, we know some ways to deal with their problems.

The first predisposed type includes species that are already becoming extinct from natural causes. These species are the true "basket cases." A number of them exist, but any one case is bound to be controversial, and reasonable people may disagree as to whether the causes in a particular case are chiefly "natural." For example, the California condor is a species about which people debate whether its decline has been caused by natural or much more proximate human factors. In any event, approximately 1,500 genera of mammals, with all their included species, have become extinct over the last ten-million years (Webb 1984).

The second type of species biologically predisposed to extinction is more easily defined. It consists of animals perfectly well adapted to the world in which they live but possessing adaptations that become dangerous for them when man adds new pressures. Consider a population of about 35,000 gray bats (*Myotis grisescens*) in a cave in Tennessee. These animals are beautifully adapted to their environment, but they require special living conditions such as one type of cave in the summer but another type in the winter—a hard-to-find environment. To deal with these environments, gray bats have highly elaborate behaviors, social organizations, and traditions, including some that we do not fully understand. Their summer habitat involves foraging over water bodies for insects that are reared in the water. Hence, these bats are also vulnerable to water quality problems, including poisoning that can be caused by man's activities.

It is worthwhile to review a few of the more striking adaptations that, under changing conditions, can make a species vulnerable to extinction. One is large body size. Large animals require many resources to support them. As a result, they tend to be rare under normal conditions; the humpbacked whale (*Megaptera novaeangliae*) is an example. Another potentially dangerous adaptation is a high trophic level, which is either high placement on a food pyramid or at the end of a food web. Because energy transfers are inefficient, and because of the added risks to intermediate species, large carnivores occurring at the top of food webs are inherently rare. High trophic level species are not necessarily large in body size, though they often are.

A third quite dangerous adaptation is seen in species that are, in biological parlance, "K-selected"—that is, they have a conservative population performance geared to a stable environment. These species have long lives, breed slowly, and pass a long time period between generations. The net effect of this is that when their numbers are severely reduced, it takes a very long time for their populations to recover. Once such a species becomes rare, it is in trouble because an additional problem can easily push it over the brink.

A fourth adaptation is seen in species with narrow habitat requirements usually related to feeding requirements. A good example is the Hawaiian honeycreeper (*Himatione sanguinea sanguinea*), a bird that feeds primarily on nectar and is inextricably linked with the botanical species that supply it with food. Its food occurs in patches, and this bird specializes in finding just those patches and making a living off them. Species having narrow habitat requirements related to feeding are usually small in body size.

Now consider the third category containing species that are vulnerable but do not have any particular predisposition to extinction. An example is the American crocodile (*Crocodylus acutus*), which has been in existence for a very long time. These crocodiles are now vulnerable because they are in man's way. The reasons are many: commercial exploitation, habitat loss, and simple extermination as feared creatures in our environment. Because such species are not biologically predisposed to extinction, biological knowledge alone is insufficient for us to understand and deal with their vulnerability. The major additional category of expertise required is management of human land use. Thus, we must understand both the biology of the beast and what man is doing with the world around him. With that additional knowledge, the answers to questions of vulnerability may become rather simple. For instance, if a major type of habitat is to be affected by man's activity, then the question is, very simply, "what lives there." But reaching agreement on solutions is an intractable matter, for we seldom can predict the effects of human land use until after the land is "converted" to its new use.

While these three catagories of vulnerable species may be easily recognized, the array of cases we now have before us is staggering, and enormous problems exist in learning to grapple with them.

FACTORS THAT INCREASE VULNERABILITY

Now let us examine three biological circumstances that lead to extinction because it is crucial that we understand how these phenomena proceed.

The first is initial rarity. Over a period of time, initially rare life forms are more likely to become extinct than initially abundant forms (Terborgh and Winter 1980).

A second factor is the smallness of the habitat available to a species. As the available area becomes smaller, the percent of existing species in it that will go extinct increases (Wilcox 1980). This simple relationship has enormous implications. Recently, we have heard a great deal about the loss of the tropical rainforests. We can rightly warn of the implications of this loss because we can look at our experience of losing most of our temperate North American forests during the last 150 years, which resulted in the attendant loss of animal species. Quite aside from the simple relationship of area to extinction, another significant element is the nature of the areas lost. Different species have different habitat requirements, and a habitat mosaic is required if an entire association of species is to be retained. As area fragmentation occurs, the smaller-sized remnants cannot contain the region's array of habitats, so they cannot support its full complement of species (Harris et al. 1982)) The consequences of this area relationship and the habitat requirements of the creatures nestled within it make it possible for us to predict faunal collapse trajectories by relating the initial number of species to the size of the shrinking and increasingly fragmented reserves and parks (Soule et al. 1979). The percent of species predicted to be lost is enormously high both in the short- and long-run. If these projections are realistic, we have a very large task ahead.

We might consider some close-to-home illustrations of these principles by recalling Jerry and Ana, who carved their names on that unfamiliar tree in a park in Florida. The park is a preserve, a fragment of the original environment. Figure 2 illustrates the way this area has changed, based on a 1973 aerial photo that shows the highway connecting the Florida mainland to Key Largo. To the south, habitat fragmentation was by 1973 virtually complete. Today the park still contains several poisonwood trees, but the Key Largo woodrat (*Neotoma floridana*) is absent. To the north, habitat fragmentation is just beginning, and in the upland forests the woodrat is abundant. A site indicated in Figure 2 has been chosen by government natural resource stewards to establish a refuge for the American crocodile that we discussed earlier. The venture is good in the sense that the American crocodile would have accessibility to a fairly sizeable tract of wetland habitat consisting of mangrove swamps. This would be a good place for crocodiles to have a refuge, but the area is much too small to support Florida panthers (*Felis concolor coryi*, Figure 3) if they were intro-

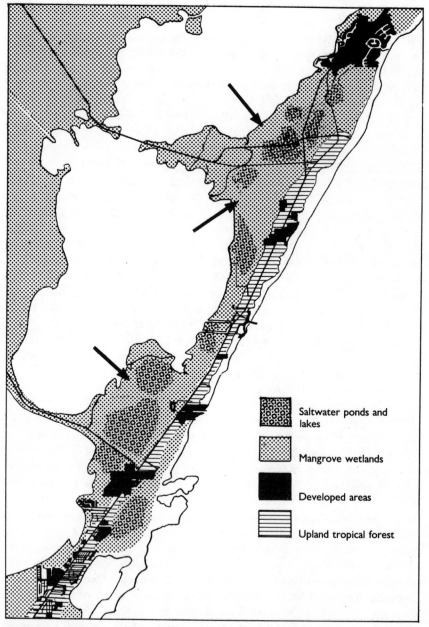

Figure 2   *A sketch of Key Largo based on a 1973 aerial photograph. From the lower left, U.S. Route 1 connects the mainland to the key. The arrows indicate sites where wildlife managers wish to establish refuges for the American crocodile. Illustration by Kathleen Spagnola.*

Table I   A comparison of juvenile survivorship between inbred and noninbred young in small populations of mammals in zoos. The evidence indicates that deleterious effects of inbreeding are widespread under conditions in which small populations are isolated genetically. Examples from Ralls et al. (1979) and Ralls and Ballou (1983).

Species	Survival	Number of young (% died noted)	
		Noninbred	Inbred
Indian elephant (Elaphas maximus)	Lived	11	2
	Died	2 (15%)	4 (67%)
Pygmy hippopotamus	L	139	23
(Choeropsis liberiensis)	D	45 (24)	28 (55)
Eld's deer (Cervus eldi thamin)	L	13	0
	D	4 (24)	7 (100)
Sable antelope (Hippotragus niger)	L	18	3
	D	4 (18)	7 (70)
Dorcas gazelle (Gazella dorcas)	L	36	17
	D	14 (28)	25 (60)
Japanese serow (Capricornus crispus)	L	52	27
	D	21 (29)	35 (56)
Short bare-tailed opossum	L	140	9
(Monodelphis domesticus)	D	2 (1)	2 (18)
Elephant shrew	L	122	33
(Elephantulus rufescens)	D	22 (15)	10 (23)
Degu (Octodon degus)	L	59	39
	D	7 (11)	12 (24)

duced. To use this available area to deal with the problem of panthers clearly is a hopeless task. This is the sort of judgment that concerned scientists and citizens need to be able to make.

The third biological process leading to extinction has to do with inbreeding depression. This is a loss of genetic diversity and is the process Dr. Challinor referred to as his major concern regarding zoos. Table 1 shows the results of research by scientists at the National Zoo. The studies revealed that inbred young have higher mortality rates than those not inbred (Ralls et al. 1979). The frightening implication is that genetic bottlenecks in captivity or in the wild can cause small populations to lose most of

Figure 3   *The Florida panther (Felis concolor coryi).*
Illustration by Kathleen Spagnola.

their adaptive variability. We therefore must have some knowledge of the genetic diversity of a species and of the number of individuals necessary for the long-term preservation of a population in order to make species' conservation a realistic business (Frankel and Soule 1981).

We noted earlier that the Florida panther cannot make it on Key Largo. The next question is whether it can make it at all. At best estimate, only about 25 of these southeastern cougars have survived. Though the animals used to live throughout the Southeast, their habitat has contracted to the swamps of southwestern Florida. We do not know whether these 25 animals carry all of the genetic material required for panther survival. As a rule of thumb, the minimum number of individuals needed for a species to maintain its adaptability is 50. However, we must recognize that the question of whether such a figure is accurate depends entirely on whether a species such as the panther has survived, through prior events, one or more earlier genetic bottlenecks. If so, the genes of the panther may contain little variation, and the remaining animals could be weakened in reproductive capability. On the other hand, this animal may survive with limited genetic variation. We do not know in this case, and the point is that we must use biological research to make such a determination for each threatened species on a case-by-case basis.

WAYS TO MEET THE CRISES

Now having looked at the processes, consider the practical question of how we can use this knowledge of biology and human land use to meet extinction crises. These crises can be approached in two ways. The first is crisis management to prevent rare species from going extinct. The second is preventing crises, which means finding out how to prevent species from becoming rare in the first place. Let me address crisis management first. Because endangerment is not predictable from theoretical knowledge alone, we must be prepared to handle problems flexibly as they emerge. For this we need an administrative process containing six components. We must have information on what is happening and we must have a formal process for identifying problems. We must decide which problems are to be solved—if they can be—and we must have workable solutions and the human and financial resources to implement them. Finally, we must find a way to resolve conflicts between conservation and development. Biologists tend to ignore this sixth point, but we really cannot afford to do so. I submit that we have three great institutions at our disposal, and that meeting the crises depends on our skill at putting them to work. These institutions are: wildlife management technology, the democratic process, and the Endangered Species Act.

Wildlife management technology is the relevant version of the scientific method: we study nature, we learn its patterns and underlying mechanisms, and we then apply that knowledge to solve specific problems. This method works when we use it fully. Hence, wildlife management technology provides some solutions, some information on what is happening, and some of the criteria for decision making. These, in turn, are provided in large part because of the success of our institutions of higher education and of biological research, including the National Zoological Park and the Smithsonian Institution. Wildlife management technology also is successful largely because of the resources of our research and stewardship agencies in state and federal governments, including the U.S. Fish and Wildlife Service's Cooperative Research Units, which link government and educational institutions.

I include the democratic processes because, although familiar, they are often forgotten in this context, despite the fact that they are crucial. In a democracy, human activities that affect both environments and citizens cannot normally be undertaken in secret because the information usually can be obtained through public records. Democratic processes provide inputs for resolving conflicts between conservation and economic interests. Our job is to put these processes to work as fully as we do the scientific method.

The Endangered Species Act formally identifies problems through the listing process. It also provides decisions on recovery efforts and priorities. Most importantly, it provides most of the financial resources we need to implement solutions.

After a decade of operation, several amendments were included in the 1982 reauthorization process for the Endangered Species Act. Some of these amendments deserve mention because they are particularly germaine to the biological nature of endangerment. One is that the new language removes all nonbiological criteria from the species listing process. This is important because the listing process is fundamentally concerned about discovering and formally recognizing problems. Therefore, this process should be relatively nonpolitical. Second, the new language requires a petitioner requesting a species listing or delisting to submit substantial evidence for his or her case. This is desirable because it prevents us from wasting our energies on spurious proposals, either for or against listings. Third, specified deadlines for decisions by the secretary of the Department of Interior are required in the listing and delisting process. This ensures an accurate and current shopping list of problems, which will be aided further by a provision saying that a listing decision can be made even if critical habitat cannot be determined at the time of the listing. The critical habitat, however, must be designated within six months. The advantage of this requirement is that the problem can be formally recognized before the land involved is identified in detail—a question obviously going beyond biological considerations. Yet specification of critical habitat cannot be postponed indefinitely.

Another amendment of great interest will set priorities for recovery plans. Recovery plans are, of course, the real actions. Until the recovery phase occurs, nothing is actually done. All the rest is talk. This amendment mandates an orderly process of deciding which actions will be taken first. And one of the top priorities is that when a conflict between conservation and development occurs, decisions need to be made about that controversy first. This is advantageous for two reasons: it preserves the democratic trust for those whose oxes will be gored, and it produces a quick decision on whether or not a solution is politically feasible. If the issue proves intractable, and a lot of time and effort and money is wasted before the impasse is reached, attention is diverted from other problems on which progress could have been made.

The Congressional Conference Report on the 1982 amendments directed that the Fish and Wildlife Service use a scientifically based priority system for listing endangered species, and that the listing not consider judgments about whether a species is a higher or lower life form. It forces the service to allow biologists in the Office of Endangered Species to replace the malformed listing guidelines announced in 1981 (which included an irresponsible definition of degree of threat and a personal perception of the relative socioeconomic value of the world's life forms) with new guidelines (U.S. Fish and Wildlife Service 1983) that establish rational priorities for listing and delisting species and for developing and implementing recovery plans. Listing priorities include the degree and imminence of threat and the taxonomic uniqueness of the species in question. Taxonomic status relates to the question: "Do these genes exist elsewhere?" If an entire species is endangered, then much genetic information is at risk (Sparrowe and Wight 1975). Conversely, if one population or perhaps several hundred populations of the species are threatened but the whole gene pool is not, there is less overall degree of risk. Accordingly, the listing priority guidelines rate a species above a subspecies and a monotypic genus above a species, degree and imminence of threat being equal. These guidelines can be applied evenhandedly to any organism.

RANKING THE SUPPORT REQUIREMENTS OF ENDANGERED SPECIES

Do the biological processes involved in extinction suggest additional criteria? The answer is clearly affirmative, but more specific biological criteria cannot be applied across taxa such as to both animals and plants. For example, the following analysis shows that "some animals are more equal than others" (George Orwell in *1984*), but the analysis cannot be applied to animals other than mammals and birds. Several factors determining vulnerability can be measured across a wide array of species, and these can be used to rank the problems to be solved. One is the metabolic cost of body size, which we can quantify as mass (body weight) to the 0.75 power (McNab 1974). Another is trophic level. We know that consumption is only about 2 percent efficient (Fleharty and Choate 1973)—that is, 2 percent of the energy in corn is converted into energy by a cow, and 2 percent of the remaining energy is converted from the cow to a human, if all the costs are counted. A third is population growth rate. We can measure population growth rate many ways, but it is proportional to generation time that can be applied across species. The fourth and last is complex: habitat specialization. Biologists currently do not know how to quantify this factor except on a case-by-case basis. The first three criteria—metabolic cost of body size, trophic level, and efficiency of energy conversion—enable us to evaluate degrees of vulnerability across species lines. We can put these into a number of equations and try to compute the "equivalent populations" of sperm whales and San Francisco Bay salt marsh harvest mice.

Equation 1 is a crude but instructive approximation:

$$\text{Equivalent populations} = \left[\frac{0.02^{(\text{Consumer level} -1)}}{m^{0.75}} \right] n$$

is more simply expressed as:

$$\frac{\left[\dfrac{(\text{Consumer level -1})}{2\% \text{ Conversion efficiency}}\right] \text{n}}{\begin{array}{c}\text{Metabolic cost of body}\\ \text{wgt. (m) to the 0.75 power}\end{array}}$$

For example, the salt marsh harvest mouse has a mean body weight of 12 grams (0.012 kg) and is a herbivore, which is assigned a consumer level of 1. A population level n of 1,000 individuals can be used in Equation 1 to standardize the comparisons.

Equivalent populations of the harvest mouse:

$$= \frac{\left[0.02^{(1-1)}\right] 1,000}{.012^{0.75}} = \frac{1,000}{.03626} = 27,579$$

Using Equation 1, a series of mammal and bird values are calculated for estimating the relative ecological rarity as a function of body weight and trophic level (Table 2). These values are 1,000 times the energy coefficients because the equations were calculated for populations of 1,000.

The 66 native mammals and birds listed by the U.S. Fish and Wildlife Service as endangered or threatened are ranked by their priority of vulnerability in Table 3. The table illustrates that the highest priority species, the sperm whale, is so much harder to support than the lowest ranking species, the salt marsh harvest mouse, that only about one-trillionth of a sperm whale exists for every mouse, given equal areas of habitat.

Predictably, whales are at the top of the priority list as very rare, expensive animals that require an enormous share of the earth's resources to support them. They are large, occupy a high trophic level, and are very long-lived. In contrast, at the bottom of the list are small species that have short lives and tend to feed on plants. Indeed, the salt marsh harvest mouse is way down at the bottom, along with the honeycreeper, the Morro Bay kangaroo rat, and a subspecies of a bob-white quail. Taking a cautious perspective, we must realize that many other biological factors affect the expression of the ones incorporated into the table. Its specifics, therefore, may impart a false sense of accuracy. But the included factors are paramount, so that the general pattern is real and relevant to the priority rank-

Table 2 Equivalent population sizes, weighted for body size and trophic level according to Equation 1, based on an actual population of 1,000 individuals in each cell. Tabular values can be converted into energy coefficients (for multiplication with real population counts) by dividing each by 1,000.

Body weight (kg)	Consumer level			
	1 Herbivores	2	3 Carnivores	4
0.001	177,828	3,557	71	1.4
0.01	32,623	632	12.6	0.25
0.1	5,623*	112.5	2.25	0.045
1	1,000	20.0	0.40	0.008
10	177.8	3.56	0.071	0.0014
100	31.62	0.632	0.0126	0.00025
1,000	5.623	0.1125	0.00225	0.000045
10,000	1.0000	0.02000	0.000400	0.0000080
100,000	0.17783	0.003557	0.0000711	0.00000142**

* The position in the table of the lowest ranking species, the salt marsh harvest mouse, with 27,579 as its equivalent population size.

** The position of the first priority species, the sperm whale, with a value of 0.000,000,3.

Table 3 Priority rank for mammals and birds.

Combined	Mammals	Birds	Species	Equivalent populations from Equation 1	Mean body mass (kg)	Consumer level
1	1		Sperm whale (Physeter catodon)	0.0000003	43,300	4.5
2	2		Humpback whale (Megaptera novaeangliae)	0.0000017	26,400	4.2
3	3		Blue whale (Balaenoptera musculus)	0.0000117	81,400	3.5
4	4		Finback whale (Balaenoptera physalus)	0.0000181	45,500	3.5
5	5		Right whale (Balaena glacialis)	0.000123	48,000	3
6	6		Sei whale (Balaenoptera borealis)	0.000429	43,600	2.7
7	7		Bowhead whale (Balaena mysticetus)	0.000864	48,600	2.5
8	8		Gray whale (Eschrichtius robustus)	0.00131	28,000	2.5
9	9		Jaguar (Panthera onca)	0.212	90	2.3
10	10		Eastern cougar (Felis concolor cougar)	0.231	135	2.2
11	11		Southern sea otter (Enhydra lutris nereis)	0.259	24.2	2.5
12	12		Florida panther (Felis concolor)	0.378	70	2.2
13	13		Gray wolf (Canis lupus)	0.940	35	2.1
14	14		Hawaiian monk seal (Monachus schauinslandi)	1.03	250	1.7
15	15		Brown/Grizzly bear (Ursus arctos horribilis)	1.19	205	1.7
16	16		Red wolf (Canis rufus)	1.21	25	2.1
17		1	Bald eagle (Haliaeetus leucocephalus)	1.27	4.89	2.4
18	17		Ocelot (Felis pardalis)	1.63	10	2.2
19		2	Calif. condor (Gymnogyps californianus)	3.82	9.1	2
20	18		Margay (Felis wiedii)	4.02	8.5	2
21	19		Jaguarundi (Felis yaguaroundi cacomitli)	4.20	8	2
22	20		Mexican grizzly bear (Ursus arctos nelsoni)	5.24	230	1.3
23		3	American peregrine falcon (Falco peregrinus anatum)	7.16	0.823	2.3
24		4	Brown pelican (Pelecanus occidentalis)	7.82	2.525	2
25	21		Wood bison (Bison bison athabascae)	7.86	640	1
26–27	22–23		San Joaquin kit fox (Vulpes macrotis mutica)	10.1	2.5	2
26–27	22–23		Northern swift fox (Vulpes velox hebes)	10.1	2.5	2
28		5	Whooping crane (Grus americana)	10.3	6.85	1.8
29	24		West Indian manatee (Trichechus manatus)	11.2	400	1
30	25		Black-footed ferret (Mustela nigripes)	20.2	0.99	2

No.			Species			
31	6		Ivory-billed woodpecker (Campephilus principalis)	22.4	0.510	2.1
32	7		Laysan duck (Anas laysanensis)	24.6	0.450	2.1
33	8		Manx shearwater (Puffinus puffinus)	35.8	0.460	2
34	9		Everglade kite (Rostrhamus sociabilis plumbeus)	42.0	0.372	2
35	10		Light-footed clapper rail (Rallus longirostris levipes)	44.7	0.342	2
36		26	Columbian white-tailed deer (Odocoileus virginianus leucurus)	55.7	47	—
37		27	Sonoran pronghorn (Antilocapra americana sonoriensis)	62.9	40	—
38		28	Key deer (Odocoileus virginianus clavium)	76.1	31	—
39	11		Red-cockaded woodpecker (Picoides (= Dendrocopos) borealis)	132	0.048	2.1
40	12		Akiapolaau (honeycreeper) (Hemignathus wilsoni)	192	0.029	2.1
41–42	13–14		Dusky seaside sparrow (Ammospiza maritima nigrescens)	172	0.020	2.2
41–42	13–14		Cape Sable seaside sparrow (Ammospiza maritima mirabilis)	172	0.020	2.2
43	15		Mississippi sandhill crane (Grus canadensis pulla)	202	5.0	1.1
44		29	Hawaiian hoary bat (Lasiurus cinereus semotus)	254	0.020	2.1
45	16		Eskimo curlew (Numenius borealis)	257	0.450	1.5
46–47	17–18		Hawaiian creeper (Oreomystis (= Loxops) mana)	332	0.014	2.1
46–47	17–18		Kirtland's warbler (Dendroica kirtlandii)	332	0.014	2.1
48	19		Hawaiian duck (-koloa) (Anas wyvilliana)	361	1.37	1.2
49–50		30–31	Ozark big-eared bat (Plecotus townsendii ingens)	373	0.012	2.1
49–50		30–31	Virginia big-eared bat (Plecotus townsendii virginianos)	373	0.012	2.1
51		32	Gray bat (Myotis grisescens)	428	0.010	2.1
52	20		Hawaiian goose (= nene) (Nesochen (= Branta) sandvicensis)	569	2.12	—
53		33	Indiana bat (Myotis sodalis)	627	0.006	2.1
54	21		Aleutian Canada goose (Branta canadensis leucopareia)	634	1.835	—
55		34	Delmarva Peninsula fox squirrel (Sciurus niger cinereus)	744	0.880	1.1
56		35	Utah prairie dog (Cynomys parvidens)	872	1.2	—
57	22		Attwater's greater prairie chicken (Tympanuchus cupido attwateri)	982	1.025	—
58	23		Kauai o'u (honeyeater) (Psittirostra psittacea)	1580	0.040	1.5
59	24		Hawaii akepa (Loxops coccineus coccineus)	2050	0.010	1.7
60	25		Puerto Rican parrot (Amazona vittata)	2590	0.281	—
61	26		San Clemente sage sparrow (Amphispiza belli clementeae)	3140	0.016	1.5
62	27		Merriam's Montezuma quail (Cyrtonyx montezumae merriami)	3550	0.185	—
63	28		Masked bobwhite (Colinus virginianus ridgwayi)	4150	0.150	—
64		36	Morro Bay kangaroo rat (Dipodomys heermanni morroensis)	7590	0.067	—
65	29		Palila (honeycreeper) (Loxioides (= Psittirostra) bailleui)	11,200	0.040	—
66		37	Salt marsh harvest mouse (Reithrodontomys raviventris)	27,579	0.012	—

ing of endangered mammals and birds. The pattern is confirmed by examining the home range size requirements of species whose needs are well documented (Harestad and Bunnell 1979).

HUMAN ATTITUDES

The foregoing is not intended to deny the importance of strictly human considerations but to provide a scientific basis for public policy toward natural resources. Ultimately, human perceptions are relevant, too, especially in making decisions about species recovery. What is the place of that species in the human culture? Does the whooping crane capture the public imagination? These are important questions. Another question that raises red flags is socioeconomic value, or "Can the species be marketed in any form?" For example, without the creative and imaginative "marketing" of the giant panda by the Peoples' Republic of China and several of the world's zoological parks, an effective response to the survival crisis of the giant panda probably would be impossible. Last but not least, the cost of a recovery effort must be evaluated carefully. But this issue should be considered last; if considered early it can preclude clear definition of the problem. When done last, costs are more obvious, and by then many problems have become smaller than they first seemed.

CRISIS PREVENTION

I wish to conclude by briefly addressing the alternative approach—preventing crisis. How do we prevent species from becoming rare? Unlike the resolution of survival crises, mechanisms for prevention are only weakly institutionalized except for game and commercial species. The single common denominator of endangered species is that they are rare, for whatever reason. The proximate, immediate reasons are so many as to be almost patternless. The ultimate reason is that when a species is rare its population growth rate is inherently unstable with respect to all the possible factors that could contribute to further loss. Therefore, it is highly likely that rare species will be driven to extinction. This is the way of entropy, as expressed in that cynicism called "Murphy's law": if extinction can happen, it will. This means that crisis management as practiced under the Endangered Species Act at best will be an expensive, uphill battle. At worst it will fail.

It follows that to the extent possible we should also seek to prevent rarity, for to do so should be cheaper and more likely to succeed. At least four ways are possible. One is to adopt appropriate technology for land use. This means, for example, using southeastern pine land for commercial forestry instead of planting pastures of exotic grasses. (This is an example of the lesser of two evils, with the alternative being even harder on the native fauna.) It means that the portion of the Everglades dedicated to parks and preserves is better served if the other portion converted to agriculture contains rice in the undrained marsh terrain, not dry-land sugarcane. The second way is to promote sustainable exploitation of wildlife resources: when what is good for wildlife is also good for people, we will actively prevent rarity. This axiom has guided wildlife management in North America for at least 50 years (Leopold 1933). Another way is to use imaginative marketing to realize the commercial potential of vulnerable species. This means for-profit nature centers on the peripheries of large cities, flower-identification and bird hike programs, and adult education courses. It means developing guided tours and opportunities for wildlife photography in state and national parks and preserves to increase the economic multiplier effects of tourism. It means management designed to preserve for people the free ecological services, such as stable water supply and flood control, that watershed protection provides in the form of montane and wetland vegetation. Pursuit of such methods is becoming formalized as a subdiscipline of environmental engineering (Odum 1971).

The fourth and potentially most powerful way to prevent crises involves a relatively new subdiscipline called community ecology. At present, this subject can be given only perfunctory treatment. When the basic science matures, its applications will produce a technology that could be harnessed to prevent rarity. Though too little is known to give us much predictive power, the general patterns of community interaction are known, and the underlying mechanisms are understood in concept though usually not in operational detail. In essence, the community approach accounts for the positive relationships of food to consumer, the negative relationships of predators, parasites, and competitors, and the suites, or interrelated groups of plants and animals, adapted for given sets of local conditions. Its management lesson is that a free-standing environment with its conditions intact will support its biota at little or no economic cost to humans. Consequently, using common-sense knowledge to preserve intact communities is the antithesis of using high technology to recover populations from the brink of extinction. This sensible approach is institutionalized in the wildlife refuge system of the U.S. Fish and Wildlife Service and the natural heritage program of The Nature Conservancy.

In summary, the key elements in safeguarding species vulnerable to extinction are biological knowledge, land-use knowledge, the integration of biological knowledge into crisis management, and an intellectually established but sociologically young venture to compliment crisis management with the prevention of crises.

References Cited and Additional Readings

Fleharty, E. D. and J. R. Choate.
   1973.   Bioenergetics strategies of the cotton rat, *Sigmodon hispidus*. *J. Mammalogy* 54:680–92.

Frankel, O. H. and M. E. Soule.
   1981.   *Conservation and Evolution*. New York: Cambridge University Press.

Harestad, A. S. and F. L. Bunnell.
   1979.   Home range and body weight—a reevaluation. *Ecology* 60:389–402.

Harris, L. D., C. Maser, and A. McKee.
   1982.   Patterns of old growth harvest and implications for Cascade wildlife. Trans. 47th North American Wildlife and Natural Resources Conference: 374–92.

Leopold, A.
   1933.   *Game Management*. New York: Charles Scribner's Sons.

McNab, B. K.
   1974.   The energetics of endotherms. *Ohio J. Science* 74:370–80.

Odum, H. T.
   1971.   *Environment, Power and Society*. New York: Wiley-Interscience.

Ralls, K. and J. Ballou
   1983.   Extinction: lessons from zoos. In *Genetics and Conservation: A Reference for Managing Wild Animal and Plant Populations*, ed. C. M. Schonewald-Cox, S. M. Chambers, B. MacBryde, and W. L. Thomas. Menlo Park, Calif.: Benjamin-Cummings Publishing Co., 164–84.

Ralls, K., K. Brugger, and J. Ballou.
   1979.   Inbreeding and juvenile mortality in small populations of ungulates. *Science* 206:1101–03.

Soule, M. E., B. A. Wilcox, and C. Holtby.
   1979.   Benign neglect: a model of faunal collapse in the game reserves of East Africa. *Biological Conservation* 15:259–72.

Sparrowe, R. D. and H. M. Wight.
  1975.   Setting priorities for the endangered species program. Trans. 40th
              North American Wildlife and Natural Resources Conference:
              142–56.

Terborgh, J. and B. Winter.
  1980.   Some causes of extinctions. In *Conservation Biology: An Evolution-
              ary-Ecological Perspective*, ed. M. E. Soule and B. A. Wilcox.
              Sunderland, Mass.: Sinauer Associates, 119–33.

U.S. Fish and Wildlife Service.
  1983.   Endangered and threatened species listing and recovery priority
              guidelines. *Federal Register* 48:16756–59 (April 19).

Webb, S. D.
  1984.   Ten million years of mammal extinctions in North America. In
              Pleistocene Extinctions, ed. P. Martin and R. Klein. Tucson: Uni-
              versity of Arizona Press.

Wilcox, B. A.
  1980.   Insular ecology and conservation. In *Conservation Biology: An
              Evolutionary-Ecological Perspective*, ed. M. E. Soule and B. A.
              Wilcox. Sunderland, Mass.: Sinauer Associates, 95–117.

3

Extinction As Part Of The Natural Evolutionary Process: A Paleobiological Perspective

STEVEN M. STANLEY

It is nice to be here at the National Zoo enjoying the living world for a change. Today there are probably four- or-five-million species alive in the world. Most of them are insects, which is why I say probably; many insects have not been observed in detail, recognized as species, or given names. A hundred times this number of species—perhaps some 450 million—have lived during the entire history of the earth. We can make this estimate because we know that an average species survives for about five- or ten-million years. The number of species that has existed at any given time since higher life forms arose has probably not different greatly from the number that exist today (lower animals have been represented by large numbers of species for hundreds of millions of years). Thus, huge numbers of species that have existed through geologic time are no longer with us.

I have often contemplated the very striking fact that for almost any species that became extinct long ago, we simply do not know the cause of extinction. Frequently, we can erect good hypotheses. Sometimes, for example, we can see evidence that competing species entered a region or that very adept predators appeared on the scene, but usually we simply do not know for sure. Often a number of factors have conspired to "do in" a particular species. When a species becomes rare, any one of a number of agents or a combination of agents can cause its extinction.

We can certainly say that extinction is a normal process. Today, however, the process of extinction is operating at an abnormally high rate. We might wonder how some of those species with the characteristics that Dr.

Humphrey has described—characteristics that make them vulnerable to extinction—have survived at all and why they are still here in substantial numbers. As it turns out, many of the characteristics that make a particular species vulnerable to extinction also make it likely to produce descendent species that bear similar features. If we think of species in the context of genera (clusters of similar species that are closely related) or families or still higher categories of classification, we must recognize that many of these higher taxa (for example, families) survive, and in fact thrive, not by virtue of including species that are immune to extinction but because they offset their normally high extinction rates with high rates of speciation—that is, high rates of production of new species. In the modern world, unfortunately, many groups that have survived by virtue of compensatory speciation simply are not going to have time for salvation by this mechanism. The same kinds of interference by humans that are now causing abnormally high rates of extinction are also shutting off or reducing rates of speciation. Thus, humans are wielding a double-edged sword.

I want now to move back into the geologic record to look at what went on long before our own species, *Homo sapiens*, walked the earth. We can somewhat arbitrarily divide geologic intervals into two groups with regard to extinction: intervals that have had "normal" rates of extinction and intervals characterized by "mass" extinction. A mass extinction is a strong, widespread pulse of extinction, one that has a major effect on the ecosystem and that generally eliminates higher taxa or large segments of higher taxa. To contrast these two kinds of intervals, I want to look at the history of marine mollusks (animals bearing seashells) for the last few million years. Figure 1 displays two graphs, one representing bivalve mollusks (oysters, clams, scallops, mussels, and their relatives) and the other representing gastropods (snails). These are all marine forms. The triangles and circles on the graphs represent ancient faunas, or fossil assemblages, that lived in California and Japan; the circles are for California, and the solid triangles are for Japan. The geologic age of a fauna is shown on the horizontal axis, and plotted on the vertical axis is the percentage of species in a fauna that survives to the present day. In other words, to plot a point on one of these graphs we must collect a group of fossils from a particular formation and then tally the species within that fauna that are alive today. The age of the fauna is determined independently by comparing it with other fossil groups or by means of radiometric dating. Indirectly, we always have some estimate of absolute age in millions of years. As we would expect, looking at older and older faunas we find there are fewer and fewer surviving species in either of these classes of mollusks. What we see represented in these graphs for the past 20-million years or so seems to be a record of "normal" extinction, with species coming and going at a kind of statistically constant rate. This is indicated both by the fact that the curves for the two areas (California and Japan) roughly coincide and by the fact that they are smooth, with no big jumps. If a sudden pulse of extinction occurred, we would expect to see a sharp downward deflection of the general band of points—this does not happen. So it looks as though around the margins of the Pacific, as exemplified by California and Japan, we have had fairly normal rates of extinction during the past 20-million years. This approximates the last third of the Age of Mammals.

When we look at the East Coast of the United States, right here in our back yard, we find something quite different. In Figure 1 the diamonds represent the faunas for the eastern United States. The sizes of the symbols represent the sizes of the faunas, and we can see that very large fossil faunas are known from the Chesapeake Bay region on down into Florida. The graphs show that these large faunas have very few living species. Typically, the faunas that are about three- or four-million years old contain between 20 and 30 percent living species when one would expect them to contain 60 or 70 percent living species. Few living representatives of the species are found in the Coastal Plain faunas near Washington, D.C. What one finds here and in the South are spectacular fossil assemblages that consist chiefly of extinct mollusks. An example is the fauna of the Pinecrest sands of Sarasota, Florida—a fauna that is about three- and-one-half million years old. It is chock full of beautiful seashells, many of them still remarkably shiny, but only about 20 percent of the species are still alive. Ironically, if we want to collect seashells along the East Coast of the United States or in the Caribbean, we are better off doing so on dry land than along a beach. A decimation of the western Atlantic fauna has occurred, and by using some arithmetic one can show that approximately two-thirds or three-fourths of all the species that lived before the Ice Age disappeared during a brief interval of geologic time. Exactly how brief we are not sure because we do not have good stratigraphic data. But what we do have is clear evidence that a mass extinction of western Atlantic marine life has occurred very recently. This event was not recognized for a long time because people assumed that many of the western Atlantic fossil faunas were quite old simply because there were so few living species within them. Only now that we have independent dating methods can we see that the faunas are quite young and include surprisingly few surviving species. Less severe pulses of extinction occurred in the North Sea (on the eastern side of the Atlantic) and also in the Mediterranean.

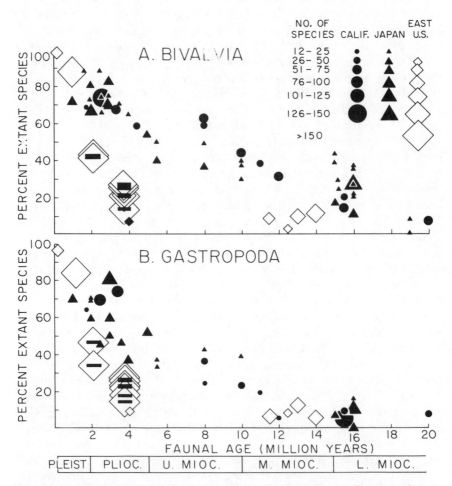

Figure I *Survival to the present of species within fossil faunas. The age of each fauna is shown on the horizontal axis and the percentage of surviving or extant species on the vertical axis. The names of the faunal ages abbreviated in the figure are: Pleistocene; Pilocene; Upper, Middle, and Lower Miocene. The horizontal black bars indicate age uncertainties for the faunas.*

All of this excessive extinction began about three-million years ago—which is not strictly the Ice Age or what we call the Pleistocene but rather the time when continental glaciation began—when huge glaciers began to spread over continents of the Northern Hemisphere. Apparently, this mass extinction came in several pulses when the glaciers expanded in between intervals of retreat. The timing of this event would suggest two hypotheses for agents of mass extinction. One possible agent would be lowering of sea level. It has often been argued that many of the major extinctions of marine life in the history of the earth occurred because sea level dropped and species were crowded together, lost habitat space, and died out in large numbers. During the Ice Age, when the glaciers spread, vast quantities of ocean water, minus the salt, were locked up as glaciers on the land, and sea level dropped perhaps three- or four-hundred feet outwards to near the edge of the continental shelves. That is one hypothesis. The other simply involves temperature reduction, or the refrigeration associated with glacial intervals. There have been a number of glacial intervals—perhaps 20 major glacial advances and retreats—during the past two-million years alone, and a few lesser oscillations occurred before that. These two hypotheses are not mutually exclusive. They might have conspired to cause the extinction. We can, however, test them against each other in a way that will possibly allow us to favor one over the other.

What we can do is look to areas of the world where sea level was lowered but little or no refrigeration occurred; areas of the Pacific Ocean, for example. There was a sea level drop here because the sea level dropped everywhere in the world, but there was not a major change in temperature during the Ice Age in California or Japan because these regions were not very close to large-scale continental glaciation. We have already seen what happened in these areas on the curves in Figure 1: there was no pulse of extinction. Species evolved and died out at a slow pace, but nothing abnormal happened. This suggests that the factor that caused the big extinction along the East Coast of the United States was a great cooling associated with the glaciation in our back yard.

Data produced by scientists associated with the international CLIMAP project, which studied deep sea cores and the fossil remains of single-celled Foraminifera that floated in the oceans, reveal the distribution of climates 18,000 years ago at the peak of the latest glacial advance. At that time, right here in the Chesapeake Bay region, a boreal climate existed and tundra lay not far to the north (Figure 2). Glaciers had descended over much of the northern part of the United States. The entire country was quite cold, with even northern Florida being temperate rather than sub-

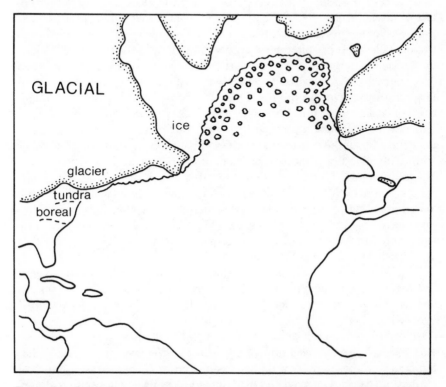

Figure 2 *Comparison of conditions in the vicinity of the northern Atlantic Ocean between 18,000 years ago and the present. Map A portrays the maximum advance of ice sheets of the most recent glacial interval, or Wisconsin Age. Map B illustrates the current configuration of continents and major ocean currents.*

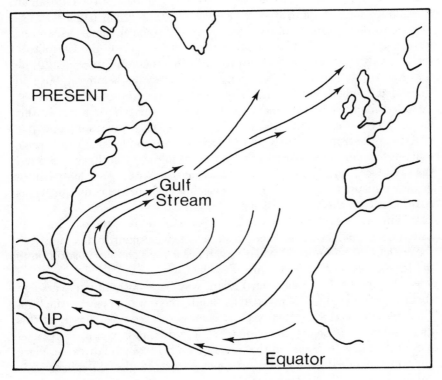

PRESENT

Gulf
Stream

IP

Equator

tropical, and the Caribbean Sea dropped significantly in temperature. It is easy to see how these conditions would have caused massive extinctions.

Another test we can make is simply to look at some of the survivors. If we consider the Florida Pinecrest fauna mentioned earlier, we find that to-day there are only about 50 species of bivalves that have survived from an enormous fauna of more than 200 species. The original fauna was ob-viously tropical in many of its characteristics. Tropical faunas, as we see, for example, in the Florida keys or in the northern part of the Caribbean, include two kinds of species with regard to temperature tolerance: those that are strictly tropical and can not live in cooler, temperate regions and those that live both in temperate regions and in the tropics. The Pinecrest included many strictly tropical species. Of the surviving species in this fauna, I have been able to find just one bivalve species that may now live strictly in the tropics. Nearly all the survivors are species that can survive temperate conditions—species that range up into the Carolinas or around the Gulf Coast to Mississippi or even Texas. So what we are left with to-day is a depauperate fauna along our coastline, which, as a consequence, is a bad area for collecting seashells!

It is my view that many of the big mass extinctions of the past have re-sulted from changes in climate. This is a somewhat unorthodox view, but the evidence is mounting. I will give you just a few examples in addition to the Ice Age event that I have just described.

At the end of the Ordovician Period, way back 450-million years ago (before vertebrate life had invaded the land), there was a major extinction. The trilobites and a number of other groups suffered major losses at this time. What happened to the climate? There was, in fact, a major glacia-tion. Just a few years ago in the Sahara Desert of North Africa—a place not widely studied geologically—people discovered glacial deposits 425-million years old, from the Late Ordovician Age. The species that died out at the end of the Ordovician Period were primarily tropical forms; species that lived at higher latitudes did not suffer so much.

Again, near the end of the Devonian Period, about 350-million years ago, there was another major mass extinction of marine life. The Devon-ian, incidentally, was the Age of Fishes when fishes rapidly expanded their ecological role as species with jaws became prevalent. The first amphibi-ans also invaded the land during this time, but their limited success left us without much of a land fauna to study. The Late Devonian mass extinction of marine life particularly affected tropical reef-dwelling creatures. They were very different animals from the ones that form reefs today. Largely because of this extinction, the fauna that had been thriving for about 150-

million years suddenly was wiped out. A map of the southern part of the world in Late Devonian time features a great supercontinent with the interesting name of Gondwanaland. It consisted of the now separate continents of Antarctica, Australia, South America, and Peninsular India. Gondwanaland at this time lay over the Late Devonian South Pole. In South America a peculiar, essentially cool-water fauna existed very close to the South Pole (largely within about 30 degrees of the Pole). This kind of fauna made it through the big extinction almost unscathed, whereas the reefs growing near the equator (for example, an enormous reef region in western Australia) underwent a massive extinction. In other areas of North America that lay close to the equator, a similar mass extinction occurred. So again we have evidence of a latitudinal control, which suggests temperature as a major agent.

What about the mass extinction that attracts the most interest—namely the one that at the end of the Cretaceous Period about 65-million years ago eliminated the dinosaurs from the earth? Dinosaurs, of course, thrived for a long period of time, and throughout the Cretaceous Period they were ruling the land. What is often overlooked is that late in the Cretaceous, in its final stage, called the Maestrichtian, dinosaurs dwindled to a point where only the horned dinosaurs, the triceratopsians, survived. The final Cretaceous mass extinction only eliminated what was left of the dinosaurs.

Many people, I am sure, have read about the idea that a meteor striking the earth may have caused the big extinction of the dinosaurs and other groups as well. The impact of such an object might have thrown large quantities of debris into the atmosphere, temporarily shielding the earth from the life-giving and warming rays of the sun. The alleged evidence for this event is a concentration of the element iridium, found particularly in Italy, at the boundary between the Cretaceous and strata representing the Age of Mammals. Iridium is extremely rare in the earth's crust but could have been introduced in unusually large quantities by an exploding meteor. Whether the "iridium spike," as it is called, is really present or well developed in other regions is debatable; people are now looking to find out. It is also unclear how common "spikes" of iridium may be at other levels of the geologic record. It is very expensive to conduct iridium analyses—this is why people are only now beginning to gather data. We also must establish whether a high concentration of iridium, wherever it occurs, is the result of low rates of sediment deposition, so that iridium is concentrated even though it was perhaps coming down to earth at a normal rate, or whether there was some extraterrestrial event that produced such a high concentration.

Quite apart from the iridium spike, which has received so much attention of late, we must recognize certain points about the mass extinction at the end of the Cretaceous Period that are often overlooked. Such a point is the evidence regarding marine plankton. There are rock sequences in southern Spain and also in Italy that include deep sea sediments that span the boundary between the Age of Dinosaurs and the Age of Mammals (between the Mesozoic and the Cenozoic Eras). In most areas, we do not have good marine sequences recording the transition because the seas fell at this time and as a result did not lay down a record for us to view above current sea level. But in the Mediterranean region, where mountain-building episodes subsequently produced the Pyrenees and the Alps, a number of deep-sea deposits have been uplifted, and a few of these include the boundary. Within these deposits we can see very clearly that the single-celled marine life that rained down on the sea floor suffered a major extinction. The forms that died out were essentially tropical forms of the Mediterranean region; they were replaced by a small number of species from which additional species later evolved. In other words, there was a reexpansion of life following the extinction event.

Thus, there is evidence of a mass extinction at the very end of the Cretaceous Period not only on the land but also in the sea. On the other hand, the extinction of many groups at the end of the Cretaceous followed a prior interval of decline. The ammonites—those very important marine fossils of the Age of Dinosaurs that essentially were squid-like animals with shells—are an example. They declined over a period of time, just as the dinosaurs did, during the last few million years of the Cretaceous.

There also were groups that declined suddenly but before the very end of the period, such as the rudist bivalves. These were remarkable, coral-like bivalves that formed enormous reefs. They were rather like oysters that attached to each other and to other creatures on the sea floor, but they grew upright with a conical lower valve. They appear very definitely to have displaced corals from the reef environment. The modern kinds of reef corals were alive in the Cretaceous Period, but as the rudist bivalves evolved, it seems they pushed the corals into the wings, where they waited, eventually to return when the rudists became extinct. Thus, it was only at the end of the Age of Dinosaurs that the corals reclaimed the reef environment. Disappearing with the rudists were other animals that lived with them in tropical seas. But the disappearance of the rudists and their tropical associates occurred before the very end of the Cretaceous. This was two- or three-million years before the so-called "iridium spike" came into being, or before the last dinosaurs disappeared.

We can see evidence of a sort of tropical bias—a selection against tropical forms—in other ways. For example, in Denmark, which of course was a relatively cool region, not nearly so severe an extinction of planktonic life occurred as in the Mediterranean. In the United States, shortly after the last dinosaurs died out, the so-called Cannonball Sea spread up from the Gulf of Mexico northward as far as North Dakota. The Cannonball Sea is named for the Cannonball Formation around North Dakota. The molluscan species of this early sea of the Age of Mammals are very similar to the mollusks of the Cretaceous. Many of the species present in Cretaceous seaways were present in the Cannonball deposits. In contrast, tropical marine life of the Gulf of Mexico suffered severe losses.

Now these sorts of latitudinal patterns suggest to me that temperature played an important role in the terminal Cretaceous extinctions. What we might have had were pulses of cooling; perhaps different groups had different thresholds of temperature tolerance. This may have been especially true for the tropical groups, which were affected most severely. Whether cooling affected the dinosaurs we do not know, but cooling was certainly recorded on the land. Paleobotanists have a very nice tool for evaluating temperatures, which involves the use of leaf margins of higher plants. Leaves that have very smooth margins or "entire" margins tend to be tropical or warm-adapted. Many more species in temperate regions have jagged or irregular margins. If one plots a curve on the percentages of "entire" margins against mean annual temperature for modern floras, one gets a straight line, a nice tight relationship. Applying this kind of curve to plants of the Late Cretaceous and early Age of Mammals in Wyoming and Montana, Dr. Leo Hickey, who until recently worked at the Smithsonian Institution, found a remarkable reduction in the percentage of "entire" margined species. He found a change from almost 70 percent species with "entire" margins fairly early in the Maestrichtian stage—perhaps about three-million years before the big Cretaceous extinction—to about 30 percent "entire" margins afterwards. This corresponds to a temperature decline in degrees Fahrenheit from perhaps about 70 degrees down to 50 degrees, about a 20 degree drop in mean annual temperature. This is a large temperature decrease, and we have to wonder if this was not really what was causing the extinctions. This would represent an immediate cause, a proximate agent of extinction. The ultimate cause or group of causes poses a more fundamental problem. There may have been a number of events that conspired to cause climates to deteriorate. Certainly, some sort of meteorite event may have been a final blow. However, no such event constitutes the whole story because, as we have seen, much of what happened occurred earlier.

Now let us shift our focus back toward the present. We are all fascinated by the magnificent fauna of the African savannah. This fauna seems all the more precious when we contemplate its uniqueness in the modern world. Few people appreciate that this is actually a remnant—all that is left of a much larger fauna. I refer not only to the fauna that existed before human interference but to a much larger fauna—one of a group of huge faunas that existed a few million years ago, one in Africa, one in Asia, and one in North America. Between ten- and five-million years ago, large regions of the world consisted of savannahs and open woodlands with enormous faunas of which we get just a hint of by what we see in Africa today. For example, in Eurasia, about ten-million years ago, there was the so-called "Hipparian" fauna, named for a horse; hyenas were just beginning to expand in variety at this time; elephants were also beginning to diversify in a large way. The faunas of this Eurasian region were enormous and spectacular, and similar faunas occupied North America.

What is missing, in particular, from the modern mammalian faunas, apart from the former vast numbers of species, is species of enormous body size. Going back a bit further, to the middle part of the Age of Mammals, we encounter *Indricotherium* (Figure 3), the largest known land mammal of all time. This animal would literally have stood head-and-shoulders above a modern giraffe. It was about 18-feet tall at the shoulders. Even more recently, during the Ice Age, 1.8 or 1.6 million years ago, there were many animals that to a modern observer would have looked alarmingly big. There were beavers the size of black bears wandering around the United States. There was an American bison with a six-foot horn spread roaming the American West. There were mammoths about 30 percent taller than a good-sized modern African elephant. There were wild horses the size of Budweiser's Clydesdales. And there was also an elegant animal called the Irish Elk, which really was not an elk but a deer with antlers that commonly spread to a breadth of seven feet. This spectacular animal was much larger than any living deer.

It appears that climatic deterioration with the onset of the Ice Age caused many large mammal faunas to dwindle, just as it decimated molluscan faunas in many seas. But there is also evidence of a more recent pulse of mammalian extinction. Between about 14,000 years ago and 10,000 years ago, as the ice sheets of the last glacial interval melted back, many species of large mammals disappeared from the earth. When I say "last," I mean most recent, of course, because the glaciers will be coming again. Some scientists have attributed this big extinction of large mammals to a wave of human hunters with advanced implements such as the Folsom point, a classic spearhead found preserved with North Ameri-

Figure 3   Indricotherium, *a giant, hornless relative of the rhinoceros, lived during the Oligocene and Miocene epochs, about 35- to 25-million years ago. Indricotherium reached a shoulder height of about 18 feet and is believed to have been a treetop browser. Illustration by Sally Bensusen.*

can bison ribs. These hunters spread from Eurasia across the Bering land bridge, which then connected Asia to Alaska and North America. They ultimately crossed the newly created Isthmus of Panama, which had formed just before the Ice Age, into South America. On the basis of strong evidence from radiocarbon dating, it has been proposed that this wave of human hunters caused many extinctions, especially of large animals that had small populations and were also easy to spot in plains or woodlands.

Finally, I want to discuss another case in which we humans may have primeval blood on our hands, and this is the blood of Neanderthal. Who was Neanderthal? Let me say that I am somewhat unorthodox but very firm in the conviction that Neanderthal was a separate species from our own. Traditionally, Neanderthal has been regarded as a subspecies of our species. When we compare the head of Neanderthal with the heads of *Homo erectus* and *Homo sapiens* (our own species) we see that the cranial shape of Neanderthal is really very much like that of *Homo erectus*: the brow ridges are very large; there is a long, low skull; the mouth projects forward; and there is a very weak chin compared to ours. *Homo sapiens* have a very tall, high-vaulted forehead and much weaker brow ridges. Furthermore, we do not have the projecting mouth or muzzle; we have a variably developed, but still often prominent, chin. Neanderthal differed from us in a number of other ways; for example, the shoulder blade of Neanderthal was distinctive, the pelvis had a slightly different shape, and the detailed structures of the hands were different. This last-mentioned difference has suggested to many people that Neanderthal had a much stronger grip than ours.

It is evident to me that if we looked at any other two kinds of mammals and saw in large populations this degree of difference we would regard the populations as separate species. Neanderthal is much more different in skeletal form from us, for example, than is a lion from a tiger. I suspect that there have been biases working in favor of including Neanderthal in our species. One problem is the question of brain size. Many people have not wanted to acknowledge the existence of any other species with a big brain, and, in fact, Neanderthal had a slightly larger brain than ours. This does not necessarily mean that he was smarter; the brain had a very different shape. Another problem has been the "single species" hypothesis: people have generally believed that only one species of humans or humanoids could ever have existed at one time. In fact, we now recognize overlaps among the various humanoid species in geologic time. People have said, "Well, we overlapped in time with Neanderthal and Neanderthal had a big brain, so Neanderthal had to be one of us." That is not very sound reasoning.

In any event, about 40,000 years ago a creature called Cro-Magnon, an anatomically modern human, appeared in eastern Europe, coming perhaps from Africa. In Africa, there are some early skulls of fairly modern aspect that seem to be quite old, perhaps older than 40,000 years. But the dates are problematical; the skulls are not complete, and the case is not clear. Anyway, Cro-Magnon people, which is to say modern humans, appeared in Europe about 40,000 years ago and seem to have moved westward. At the same time, Neanderthal disappeared. There was clearly an interval of overlap (the dates are good here because of the applicability of radiocarbon dating). On the face of it, it really does appear that modern humans caused the extinction of Neanderthal. This is not certain, but the circumstantial evidence is striking. Neanderthal had occupied Europe for about 70,000 years, and then *Homo sapiens* suddenly appeared on the scene, and Neanderthal disappeared. If such displacement occurred, it would be evidence that we are, in fact, a separate species from Neanderthal because as a different species we would not have assimilated them. Keep in mind that reproductive separation and inability to coexist are criteria for the separateness of species. When we include human behavior in this equation, it becomes somewhat complicated to talk about the normal distinctiveness of species. However, it is quite striking that, although Neanderthal existed for more than 70,000 years, the stone tool culture of this humanoid creature never changed very much, and Neanderthal never developed sophisticated art. In contrast, as many people are aware, the Cro-Magnon cave paintings of Europe are spectacular, and when our species appeared in Europe it was very quickly doing many sophisticated things, not only in art but also in tool use. It seems possible that Neanderthal lacked certain components of our intellect. This may have been the result of having a different kind of brain as may be indicated by the different shape of the cranium. We do not really know for sure; I tend to have a bias in that direction, but it is an area of debate between specialists.

One fact of profound significance is that Neanderthal had religion. A burial site of a young Neanderthal has been found in which stone tools were provided, apparently for use in an afterlife, and cooked meat was also left for the dead individual—charred bones are evident. There is also a site in the Middle East where Neanderthal was buried on boughs, apparently for comfort, in a sort of reclining position, and pollen analyses of the sediments have shown that the body was laid to rest with a variety of attractive flowers. So Neanderthal was humanoid, if not perfectly human, and I think it is rather important that when we consider animal extinctions, we also contemplate that we may willfully have taken the life of this evolutionary cousin of our own species.

References Cited and Additional Readings

John, B. S., ed.
  1979.   *Winters of the World: Earth Under the Ice Ages.* New York: John Wiley and Sons.

Stanley, S. M.
  1981.   *The New Evolutionary Timetable: Fossils, Genes and the Origin of Species.* New York: Basic Books.

Stanley, S. M.
  1984.   Mass extinctions in the ocean. *Scientific American* 250:64–72.

4

A Look At The Present Extinction Spasm
And What It Means For The Future Evolution Of
Species

NORMAN MYERS

I am delighted to be here to talk about the question of disappearing plant and animal species. To begin with, let me say that I want to treat the subject as an inquiry into the issue and as a challenge—not as a problem. In some respects, of course, it is a problem, but we have not yet reached the stage where the roof is falling in on us. The big spasms, or abnormal waves of extinctions, still lie a bit ahead of us. We still have, so-to-speak, a few minutes before midnight. So let us not think of it as an unsolvable problem.

I am also glad to be with you because I know that we here today are basically in agreement on the importance of the situation we are discussing. It is good to be able to talk with a group of people who, because of their presence at this symposium, are demonstrating their concern; people whom I might characterize as the "converted." And I know that if I speak about "food chains," as somebody else did this morning, you will not think I am talking about a line of grocery stores. I do wish, though, that we could also be speaking with some of the "unconverted" in this country who, I gather, according to Dr. George Gallup and some of the opinion polls, constitute a minority. Because the bulk of the citizenry in the United States apparently does believe that we should give greater priority to the question of species survival, it would be helpful to have a good dialogue with nonsupportive citizens and officials who have not yet gotten the message. We might then be able to convince them that the issue of disappearing species is of high priority and should occupy the leaders of all nations. It ranks right up front with other major issues of today such as inflation, unemployment, and stagnant productivity. Because the issue of threatened species is related to these other topics, I am going to deal with that relationship before I come to the main body of my talk.

Modern economic systems work by virtue of reliable and abundant supplies of diversified raw materials. If we have plenty of raw materials, the system works. There is no stock of raw materials on this earth that is in greater abundance and extreme diversity than the five- to ten-million plant and animal species that share this planet with us. If we were to set our minds to the task, we could use those species to support our daily lives in a myriad of additional ways. We already benefit in utilitarian fashion from many of these natural organisms. Just think, for example, of how many times today we have used natural rubber. Not only once when we came in our cars, or even a dozen times. I would think several dozen times already. And a hundred years ago, the rubber tree was considered to be a weed tree of no use to humankind. Scientists have thus far had a close look at perhaps 1 percent of the five- to ten-million species that share this planetary home with us. Yet these species already provide many thousands of products—a whole cornucopia of goods—that support and enrich our lives. Another 10 percent or less has been looked at in a cursory fashion. Consider how many more "rubber trees" are sitting out there in the Amazon rain forest or in the middle of Borneo, awaiting discovery of their usefulness to man. This is one of the economic connections to which I refer, and it indicates how the issue of disappearing species is linked with and deserves to be considered on a par with other major issues of our times.

Let me just mention two or three quick examples of some of the major benefits we derive from wild species. Other speakers will be going into this in greater detail. In California the agricultural industry has been afflicted from time to time with pests, especially insect pests, and weeds. One effective defense has been to mobilize so-called "natural enemies" of the insect pests that come along and destroy citrus and other crops. Such pests can be controlled by wasps or other natural predators or parasites. The latest figure I have from colleagues at the University of California is that the cumulative economic value of mobilizing such natural enemies during the past 48 years has now topped $770 million. This is an example of how the natural world helps us in a way we may not realize when we go out and buy citrus fruit. Without these wasps and other natural enemies, our morning glass of orange juice would most certainly cost more.

Medicine offers another example. When we take a prescription from the doctor to the neighborhood pharmacy, there is one chance in two that the medication we collect will owe its origin, in some way or another, to "start point" materials found in wild plants or animals (but chiefly in plants). The total worldwide commercial value, or cross-counter value, of these medications is now approaching $40 billion a year.

Let us examine the situation with plants in a little more detail. In ballpark figures, there are about a quarter-million plant species on the face of this planet, and 1 in 10 of these is now threatened. Scientists have found that an average of 1 out of 120 species may prove useful against high blood pressure, heart disease, or whatever. The 40 or so plant species that we now use in medicine are generating benefits of around $40 billion a year. It is possible that the earth will lose 25,000 plant species by the end of this century. If 1 out of 120 of these were to become medically useful, just imagine the loss if those 200 plants go under. According to my arithmetic, rudimentary as it is, the potential loss to society could be hundreds of billions of dollars a year through just those plant extinctions. I should mention here that I owe the basic data behind these estimates to Norman Farnsworth of the College of Pharmacy of the University of Illinois in Chicago. He has produced some compelling economic figures to justify the preservation of species.

Still another example relates to petroleum. There are various trees that do not so much produce carbohydrates in their tissues as they do hydrocarbons. We know that hydrocarbons are what make up petroleum. When the day comes when we cannot pump any more oil out of the ground because we have used it all up, we might find that we can turn to petroleum plantations as a source of fuel, provided that the right tree species are still in existence. And a petroleum plantation need never run dry like an oil well.

This introduction is intended to outline some of the economic repercussions of the massive spasm of extinctions that is just a little bit down the road from us. How big, in fact, is the anticipated spasm? I mentioned earlier that we share the planet with somewhere between five- and ten-million other species. The number can only be estimated. Some scientists say that there are less than five million, and some say there are a good deal more than ten million. An entomologist at the Smithsonian Institution here in Washington, D.C., Dr. Terry Irwin, believes, on the basis of some very interesting evidence, that there may be thirty-million insects alone. But let us stay with the five-million as a baseline working figure.

In the mid-1970s, when I was preparing material for my book "The Sinking Ark," I tried to get a handle on the rate at which species were, in fact, disappearing. The figure we used to hear was one species per year, but that referred primarily to mammals and birds, and only to species that were actually observed to be disappearing. But because we have identified only about one-sixth of all the existing species on earth anyway, and a multitude exists to which we have not even given names, we can reasonably assume that many more than that are going under. In looking at the distribution of species on the earth's surface, I soon found that the scientific community believes that at least two-thirds of all existing species live in the tropics. And of those two-thirds, at least one-half live in the tropical moist forests. We can thus reckon that these tropical moist forests contain nearly two-million species, even though they extend over a very small part of the earth's surface, or approximately 7 percent of the land area. Moreover, the tropical forests are taking the biggest beating right now. There are various estimates of the rate at which they are being grossly disrupted or actually destroyed. I think it is fair to say that by the end of the century we can expect that somewhere between one-third and one-half of all our remaining tropical moist forests will be so grossly disturbed or depleted as to have lost much of their capacity to support their current huge array of species. They will not, by a long way, have been destroyed altogether—a few trees will still be standing—but they will not be virgin ecosystems as they are now, able to support a remarkable variety of species.

Now if we assume that between one-third and one-half of those forests are going to be degraded for wildlife purposes by the end of the century, we can estimate that two-thirds to three-quarters of a million species are highly threatened in these tropical moist forests alone. When we include other parts of the world—such as woodlands, coral reefs, wetlands, and other areas that are especially rich in species—and consider how much of these areas we are also likely to lose by the end of the century, it seems reasonable to surmise that by the year 2000 we could lose one-million species out of the postulated minimum of five million.

What about the rate at which this could occur? If we say that one-million species will disappear in the last twenty years of this century, that averages out to more than one hundred and thirty species a day. But the big waves of extinctions are not expected to occur in the next two or three years but in the late 1990s, as human populations inexorably build up and generate their enormous impact. If we were to assume that the earth is now losing just one species per day, then it is realistic, I suggest, to suppose that by the end of the 1980s, it will be losing one species each hour; and that by the end of the 1990s, it could be losing dozens of plant and animal species with every single hour that goes by.

When I worked out these figures, I circulated the arithmetic to several hundred scientific colleagues throughout North America, Western Europe, Japan, and Africa. The consensus was that the current figure of one species a day is probably pretty cautious and conservative. Some people say 500 species a year, and some say 1,000. The figure varies. Anyone can make a guess, but there seems to be no doubt that the rate of extinction today is much greater than we would have supposed it to be just a few years ago. The rate is also very much greater than it has been since the first flickerings of life arose on the face of this planet some three-and-a-half billion years ago. We heard this morning from Dr. Stanley about the great dying—as it is sometimes called—of the dinosaurs and their kin some 65-million years ago, when more species disappeared in a short space of time than in any other period of earth's history. Apparently, the maximum rate of extinction for the dinosaurs was about 1 species every 10,000 years—a pretty low rate when compared with the current 1 species per day. So what we are facing in the period immediately ahead of us is a biological debacle, a gross impoverishment of our world on a scale greater than at any other time since life began. That is the size of it.

Now the question to be asked—and the question, I think, that government and industry leaders and some unconcerned citizens might want to ask themselves—is: Do we really want a phenomenon of that scale to occur within our lifetime? Do we want our children, grandchildren, and all who will follow us to look at these two final decades of the twentieth century and say, "How could they have done such a thing?" For what reasons did they decide that it really was worthwhile to allow all those species to perish? What were the benefits that humankind derived in exchange for their demise? These are the kinds of questions we ought to be asking right now to generate informed public debate before this predicted spasm of extinctions is allowed.

Let me say that I can foresee certain circumstances in the practical world in which we would have to decide that it is better that a particular species disappear because the benefits to humankind would be so great and so unobtainable in any other way that the trade-off would be justified. As a practical, hard-nosed conservationist, I would not be inclined to argue that we must try to save each and every existing species on earth—that is just not realistic. It is too late to begin trying to do that. However, suppose we do lose a million species in the next two decades and possibly another million or another two million during the first half of the twenty-first century. After this time the growth in human numbers might level off, and we might reach some kind of ecological equilibrium with our living space. Is there still another major issue down the road if that happens?

Well, there is. I mentioned a few minutes ago that during the whole of the planet's history there has never before been such a massive and compressed spasm of extinctions. If we now precipitate a spasm of that scale, what does it mean for the processes of evolution? Can the processes of evolution pick up the remaining bits over the next thousand or million years and restore genetic diversity? There have been various phases in prehistory when a large proportion of species has disappeared, sometimes as many as one-quarter, one-half, or even two-thirds of the existing species. And in due course, meaning 20- or 30-million years, the processes of evolution have been able to restore the diversity of life and generate new species. But this time, it may not work out like that. In the past, when an outburst of extinctions has occurred the earth has generally retained some concentrations of biological diversity, or "pools of species," from which the rest of the planet could be colonized after the geologic catastrophe had passed. This occurred on a minor scale just 20,000 years ago when the last glaciation receded, and the earth was able to restock itself with plants and animals. At that time, the main storehouse from which those plants and animals came was the tropical moist forest, a kind of repository of species from which the earth could restore itself. However, the part of the planet that is being most severely disrupted right now is precisely those tropical moist forests. So the next time, when evolution has to try to pick up the bits and restore the situation, it will very likely not have that reservoir of species with which to do the job.

Still these are considerations for the next five-, fifteen-, or thirty-million years, and we are not going to be around for quite that length of time. What about the more immediate future when we shall be in our rocking chairs and our children making their way? If we lose one- or two-million species in the near future does it really matter all that much? I suspect that it does. Dr. Stanley mentioned earlier that when a large number of species disappear, the process tends to be counterbalanced by increased speciation, an evolutionary process that throws up new species to occupy vacancies we call the ecological living space. New species can rush into that ecological living space, take up the new-found opportunity to grow, establish themselves, and flourish. Species especially good at exploiting these new opportunities tend to be creatures biologists call "r-selected"—that is, species that are highly opportunistic. They can rush in, they are highly mobile, they are adaptable, and they can very rapidly reproduce their numbers. They can take over a situation and more or less control it unless they have natural enemies in sufficient abundance to keep their own numbers down. Some examples of these r-selected species are with us in the world right now. One is the common rat (Figure 1); another the cockroach (Figure 2); another the house sparrow; and finally, the plants we choose to call

Figure 1   *The Norway rat* (Rattus norvegicus) *arrived in North America about 1775. The Norway and black rat* (Rattus rattus) *are considered to be significant pest species. The Norway rat is often found associated with human populations. Illustration by Vichai Malikul.*

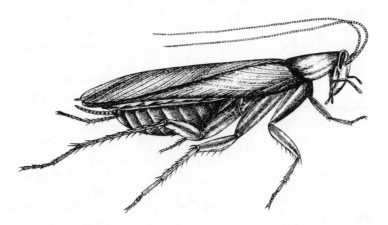

Figure 2   *The German cockroach* (Blatella germanica) *is one of the best known "pest species" that has flourished by adapting to human culture and technology. Illustration by Vichai Malikul.*

weeds, which tend to proliferate and dominate their local environments. So it is possible, even probable, that within 50 years, when many current species disappear and their places begin to be taken by others, we will have a disproportionate number of species we would characterize as "pest" or weed species. That is the kind of biological world our children are going to have to contend with. We might want to wish them luck.

So much for evolutionary perspectives. What can we do about this entire situation? I said at the beginning that the current extinction spasm is to some extent an already existing problem, but that it has not yet become an almighty problem. We can still think of it as a kind of challenge. What can we do to try to counteract the situation? Let me suggest a shopping list of initiatives that we should think about. One is that we need many more parks and reserves around the earth. The total number of protected areas now amounts to about 2 percent of the earth's land surface. Two percent is a pretty good average when you consider that in the United States the figure is only 1.6 percent, a figure that includes all the big parks in Alaska. Some countries, such as Kenya, have as much as 6 percent of their land surface set aside as parks and reserves. Tanzania, one of the most impoverished countries on earth, with a total national budget that is less than New York spends on ice cream each year, has set aside 15 percent of its total land area for parks and reserves. So these developing countries, some of them at least, are trying. In Zambia, farther south, the figure is about 25 percent. Worldwide, however, the average figure is only about 2 percent. Scientists seem to believe, estimating as best they can in an uncertain situation, that we would need 10 percent of earth's land surface before we could do even a basic job of safeguarding sufficient natural environments to keep species alive.

What are the costs? Again I present some crude and rudimentary ballpark figures: the bill to set up these parks and reserves would be about $100 million. Another $20 million would be needed annually to maintain them. That might sound like a lot, but consider that $100 million is the amount by which the total armaments bill increases worldwide from one day to another! If we were to safeguard all these species, with the abundant stocks of diversified raw materials they represent and their potential for sustaining human welfare into the indefinite future, would not the global community be interested in purchasing more security for itself than by spending the same $100 million on half-a-dozen fighter planes? Very few governments have given this question five minutes of thought. But fortunately, one or two are beginning to ponder whether there might be some mileage in this sort of analysis, which is good news.

Now how should we safeguard the tropical forests, the areas that need the most urgent attention? If we want to safeguard a sufficient area of tropical forest, it might have to be as much as 20 or even 25 percent and not the 10 percent global fraction I mentioned earlier. We might need to think in terms of one-billion dollars a year. This morning we had in our audience Dr. Ira Rubinoff, director of the Smithsonian Tropical Research Institute in Panama. Dr. Rubinoff has just written a very interesting and visionary paper suggesting that, according to his arithmetic, we may need three-billion dollars a year to sufficiently safeguard tropical forests, a preliminary but informed reckoning. Is three-billion dollars a year such a big sum? If we were to divide that figure up among the citizens of the developed countries (never mind the developing ones), it would amount to less than one martini per month per adult. Would not that sacrifice be balanced by the benefit we would get? The people in this audience, mostly parents I guess, are spending, as my wife and I are spending, many thousands of dollars on each child to bring up that child from birth through college. At the moment, we are bringing that child up into a world that is going to be greatly impoverished because it will be deprived of many species of plants and animals. Would we not reinforce our investment in that child's future by setting aside just five dollars a year, or ten dollars a year, to safeguard species that the child might want to have around when it grows up? These are some of the costs we have to think about.

Obviously, such financial support is not available right now. The cause of conservation is a very long way from having that kind of money at its disposal. In the meantime, all these species are under threat. I mentioned that one-tenth of all plants are under threat; let us say that one-tenth of all species are under threat, or half-a-million species, disappearing at a rate of one per day. Given the money we do have available, we cannot, by a long way, help all endangered species—regrettable as that may be. We have to allocate our scarce conservation dollars to the best effect possible. And that means choosing those species and ecosystems that would give us the best returns on our scarce conservation dollars. Whenever we choose to conserve a bunch of species "over here," an implicit decision is made that those species "over there," which are not getting our conservation dollar, are somehow not so "deserving" as the species we have chosen. We are assigning priorities and saying that certain species are in some way more important than others. We may not be quite sure why we are making that choice, but we are making it anyway. It is an awfully tough fact of life to face up to.

What I am talking about here is "triage," the concept Dr. Challinor discussed in his introductory address. The word is derived from the French verb meaning "to sort out." In conservation we find this term used in the sense of choosing. Now the question is not whether we should consider triage for the future because we are practicing triage right now. When any of us decides, for example, to give money on behalf of a particular species, be it a tiger, a turtle, the California condor, or whatever, we are ruling out alternative choices of giving. The case of the California condor, if I may speak about a species that belongs to your country, illustrates the impact of such choices. I have seen a lot of cost-benefit analysis that has gone into the program for the condor; a great many people have made a fine effort to work out the best way to assist that bird. The amount of money to be spent is $25 million over a period of 30 years, and the chances of success are rated at only 50-50. We should question whether we should consider spending that same amount of money on behalf of perhaps 100 species in the middle of the Amazon, for which there is a 95 percent chance of success in a conservation program and an equally good chance they will disappear if we do nothing. This is the guts of triage. Part of the question, of course, is understanding what can be done and determining through what organizations our donations can be put to use. These are topics that I believe urgently need as much informed public discussion as possible.

Sometimes I am advised by my conservationist colleagues not to talk about triage to public audiences; they fear it will give the wrong impression, that someone will say, "OK, if you want to choose in favor of the tiger or the California condor, which species are you deciding are not worthwhile and can be put over the side of the boat?" That is not the way it is at all. When I suggest that we need to choose consciously, as methodically as possible and with as much information as possible, I am not making bets about which creatures would win a beauty contest or should appear at the top of the conservationists' lists. Various magazines have asked me to write articles about this; they say, "Come up with a nice little list, Norman Myers, of species that you think we can do without." Well, I am not going to do that. My own personal philosophy is that every species, as a manifestation of creation's life force on earth, deserves to have its own chance to live out its life span—if we can possibly manage it. That gets us into the realm of aesthetics and ethics. There are other issues as well. Consider the smallpox virus, which has now been backed into a corner in a flask, so to speak, in one or two laboratories. It is being maintained at a cost of only a few thousand dollars a year, but some people would say that the smallpox virus has caused so much harm, so much misery and suffering, that we should pull the plug on the thing and eliminate it by deliberate choice. Yet it turns out that medical people are now surmising that we may, one day quite soon, establish that the smallpox virus can assist us with some of our medical research. So there is no species that on scientific, economic, ethical, or aesthetic grounds should be put over the side of the boat. That is the stand on which I will most firmly place my feet.

Unfortunately, that is not the way the world works. The amount of conservation money we have to assist threatened species is only a small fraction of what we would need to do a sufficient job. We can and must get on with the job and make the best of it. We need an open and ongoing discussion as to how we should go about making choices. And we had better start trying to assemble the necessary information to do a better job with the funds we have. I can see no greater challenge, agonizing though it will be for the conservationist community, than to start deciding right now where to put our priorities. Because with every day that goes by, with every bit of conservation planning that we do, we are, in effect, already making choices; we are already embarked on triage. We are not doing it deliberately or with systematic thought, but we are doing it. So let us start doing it as consciously and methodically as we can.

References Cited and Additional Readings

Ford, B.
    1981.   *Alligators, Raccoons, and Other Survivors: The Wildlife of the Future.* New York: William Morrow and Co.

McLoughlin, J.
    1978.   *The Animals Among Us: Wildlife in the City.* New York: Viking-Penguin.

Myers, N.
    1979.   *The Sinking Ark.* Oxford: Pergamon Press.

Myers, N.
    1983.   *A Wealth of Wild Species: Storehouse for Human Welfare.* Boulder, Colo.: Westview Press.

5

The Value Of Animal And Plant Species For Agriculture, Medicine, And Industry

E L L I O T T   A.   N O R S E

Conserving biological diversity is so very important for mankind that I am going to include all species of living things in this discussion rather than limit it to animal species. This "nonsectarian" approach will enable us to take a broader look at the topic.

Let us start with the loss of one particular animal species. The story begins when in 1741 the crew of a Russian ship discovered gigantic sea creatures in the waters around the fog-shrouded Komandorskiye Islands in the Bering Sea between Siberia and Alaska. The crew, whose unexciting diet consisted chiefly of hard-tack biscuits and dried fish, found very quickly that these gigantic, strange mammals were good to eat, and they began to kill them. Other ships followed, and within 27 years, by 1768, Steller's sea cow (*Hydrodamalis gigas*), a relative of the manatee, was extinct—gone from the face of the earth forever (Figure 1). The implications of this loss and of the enormous number of extinctions that are expected in the future are very grave if we fail to change the course upon which humankind seems so firmly embarked.

Before we examine closely why the loss of Steller's sea cow was so significant, let us gain a perspective on the time periods with which we are dealing. A fairly familiar edifice, the Washington Monument, is 555-feet tall. Let us say that its height represents the length of time during which there have been living things on this planet, around three-and-a-half billion years. Ninety percent of this immensely long period falls before the evolution of the reptiles. The period when mammals became dominant, 65-million years ago, would be represented by the top 10 feet or so of the

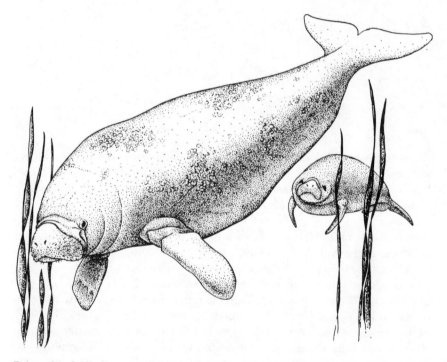

Figure I   *Steller's sea cow* (Hydrodamalis gigas). *This large relative of the manatee lived in the northern Pacific Ocean until the eighteenth century. Its demise is an example of human-caused extinction. Illustration by Sally Bensusen.*

monument. And the time from which human beings became differentiated from their ancestors, about three-million years ago, would be represented by a few inches at the peak.

Now let us change the time scale and say that the whole height of the Washington Monument represents just those three-million years of human presence on earth. Human beings began causing serious environmental impact by participating in the extinction of species in only the most recent 40,000 or so years. This period—when the earth lost the great woolly rhinoceroses, woolly mammoths, cave bears, giant ground sloths, and many other species—would, again, be represented by just the top few feet of the monument. Indeed, the period since the beginning of agriculture, some 10,000 years ago, is one during which the extinction of species has accelerated markedly.

Let us finally suppose that the whole 555-foot monument represents just that 10,000 years since the beginning of agriculture. In this case, the top few feet of the monument would represent the 130 years since the Industrial Revolution, and a few inches would represent the 18 or so years from now to the end of this century. Yet within these next 18 years, huge numbers of species that took three-and-a-half billion years to appear and accumulate on earth could be decimated. Estimates are that the total number of existing species could be cut by 10 percent, perhaps 20 percent. As Dr. Myers has suggested earlier in this symposium, the exact figures are uncertain, but what we know is this: we are going to be losing species at a rapidly accelerating rate unless we can bring about a most fundamental change in the way we do business on this planet. And the reason is people. There are too many people, given our existing level of skill and art in living on this planet and with each other.

Only a few thousand years ago, the earth's human population was miniscule; all of the people could have fit into any one of the large cities of the world today. The earth's population is now four and three-fourths billion. By the end of this century, it is projected to be six and one-third billion. We are doubling ourselves every 39 or 40 years. And not only is the increase in the number of people of concern; each person naturally wants a larger and larger portion of the earth's resources. Our reproductive rate is exceeded by other species in nature; but in nature, other organisms have checks and balances on their populations. This is the big difference between our situation and that of other species. And because there is no more dominant species on this planet that holds our numbers in check, we must decide to check ourselves or some other mechanism will take over for us. This is very difficult to do. People love having children. People love bringing forth new life. The tragedy is that this new life, especially in developing countries, is condemned to live in poverty. An ever-larger fraction of people are going to live in misery unless we have the courage and wisdom to gain control of the situation.

Now what does the pressure of human population have to do with species extinctions? What does it have to do with the loss of Steller's sea cow? Many would maintain that, as a part of the natural world, Steller's sea cow had a right to live. These gigantic, magnificent creatures would, they believe, have enriched all of us in one way or another. Some may conceive this as a basic, ethical premise, but others do not buy this argument. They say that if the value of a species cannot be shown in dollars and cents, they do not want to hear about it.

Two basic arguments for the preservation of species can and should persuade such people that it is against their own interests, and the interests of everyone, to allow extinctions to occur. The first is the role of individual species in the functioning of ecological systems or "ecosystems." Dr. Ehrlich will be speaking about that later in this symposium. Without anticipating his presentation, let me indicate the importance of this topic. In every glass of water we drink, some of the water has already passed through fishes, trees, bacteria, worms in the soil, and many other organisms, including people. We have a finite amount of water on this planet, and its quality is going to be a matter of increasing interest and urgency as the years go by. Living systems cleanse water and make it fit, among other things, for human consumption and for the needs of other species. Trout are even fussier in their needs than we are. That is why trout have told us something by disappearing from lakes in large areas of upstate New York and Canada. Their disapperance apparently has been caused by acid rain from our industrial activities.

The role of a species in an ecosystem is very important, and it turns out that the Steller's sea cow was a keystone species in the waters of the Aleutian Islands, the Komandorskiye Islands, and all around the cold Pacific Coast of North America, where it dwelt before it was driven toward extinction. Steller's sea cow grazed on the giant algae that lived in the coastal waters, something that very few other organisms do. In so doing, it opened up patches that were then exposed to sunlight so that different kinds of algae could grow and different animals could feed on and hide among the algae. Thus, Steller's sea cow had a major role in bringing about the community structure—the array of interdependent organisms in those ecosystems. But now they are gone, and we will never really understand what those ecosystems were like.

As it happens, the second basic argument for conserving species is also illustrated very well by Steller's sea cow. This is that individual species can be put to direct use by people. Steller's sea cow tasted like fine veal. Its fat was said to be better than the finest butter. So what we had, if we want to be perfectly crass about it and forget the fact that this was a magnificent creature, was a ten-ton animal that was both superb tasting and grew on pastures that we human beings do not use—pastures in the sea. The Steller's sea cow could have probably expanded the food supply for humankind. But we botched it. We killed a goose that could have laid golden eggs.

AGRICULTURAL USES

I would like to emphasize the second point, the direct usefulness of species for human purposes, beginning with agriculture. The United States is a world powerhouse in food production. The farmlands of the American Midwest are of major importance in the world's food balance. Thus, the methods by which we produce food grains in the United States have some very serious consequences. When we take a bite of a loaf of bread, we are really taking a bite of oil because the tractors that plow the ground, the insecticides used to suppress crop pests, the herbicides used to keep down weeds, and the fertilizers used to accelerate plant growth are all derived from or are heavily dependent upon petroleum and other fossil fuels. These methods of agriculture have been developed very recently yet are essentially temporary because fossil fuels are running out, and they are not renewable. We are not going to be able to keep up this mode of agriculture forever.

Through the management of living resources, we have a potential means of stretching out our agricultural productivity for the future. In living resources, I include not only the familiar organisms such as mammals, birds, and plants, but also bacteria that live in the soil and "fix" nitrogen, turning it into a useful fertilizer for plants. This also includes beneficial insects that could control insect pests that now drain off a significant portion of the world's agricultural productivity.

Examples of potential new food sources can be found in plants, animals, and fishes. For example, one is the sea grass called eel grass (*Zostera marina*) because of its serpentine, eel-like appearance. It produces a grain and lives along the temperate coasts of much of the world, from New Zealand to Alaska. We once had a lot of eel grass in the Chesapeake Bay, but runoff from farmers' fields surrounding the bay contains fertilizers that have encouraged the growth of tiny algae in the water and shaded out the eel grass. Eel grass seeds have been used for several hundred years by a group of Indians on lands bordering the Gulf of California. Because we grow very little plant food from the sea, and virtually no starchy food, this could be a potentially useful source of food for us in the future.

The American bison, or buffalo, is another example. It supported populations of Plains Indians in the United States for many years. When Europeans came to America, they brought with them European cattle, European goats, European sheep, and other familiar animals and plants from the Old World. To them, the buffalo was a strange and, because Indians ate it, somewhat forbidding creature. But the interesting thing is that buffalo are better adapted to the native conditions of North American grasslands than are European cattle. When buffalo are cross-bred with our domestic cattle, the resulting animal is one that reaches market weight twice as fast as our cattle and has a lower percentage of body fat. This could have been a significant addition to our food supply that might have reduced the intake of animal fats among Americans. Bison meat, however, has never been met with widespread acceptance.

Fisheries provide a third example. Potential exists for cultivation of many kinds of marine and freshwater organisms, including trout in the temperate zones to fishes that live in the Amazon River and eat leaves and fruits that fall from trees. The people of China get a significant amount of their protein from fish, and a major fraction of those fish are grown in ponds in China and in lagoons along its coastline. Aquaculture of fin fish and shellfish could have considerable potential for augmenting food supplies were it not for two things: first, we are very rapidly polluting the inland and coastal waters that would be the best locations for aquaculture, rendering them useless for this purpose; and second, we are pushing more and more species toward extinction, again killing the "goose that laid the golden eggs." Fishes are disappearing very quickly. For example, one of the largest fish found in the western United States, the Colorado squawfish (*Ptychocheilus lucius*), is on the federal Endangered Species List. It was formerly abundant and a major food source of Arizona and Colorado Indian tribes. But the free-flowing western rivers it needs to survive have been dammed up. Its habitat has been so reduced that it is now on its way out, even though we are doing everything we can to save it.

Another interesting and most surprising example has come to light. Cheese is rather expensive now. It is made using rennet, an enzyme from the stomachs of calves or sheep that is in limited supply. We just cannot get enough rennet to make the quantity of cheese people demand. Scientists are now finding that rennet-like substances occur in the stomachs of fishes, and that we can make cheese using those substances. There is even an energy advantage in doing so because the enzymes from cattle must be kept at about 37 degrees centigrade, or at body temperature, to work effectively. But because a number of these fishes live in rather cold water, where their stomach enzymes must function, heating would not be so necessary.

Waste is a significant problem in many fisheries. I have been on shrimp trawlers and been absolutely appalled by the amount of good food that is wasted. Living resources are brought on deck, allowed to die, and then shoved back into the water. Perhaps only 1 or 2 percent of a catch is shrimp, while much of the remainder is other kinds of edible fin fish and shellfish. Our standard fishing method right now is to throw everything but the shrimp back into the sea, dead. This is very, very wasteful. In a world of hungry people, some might even say it is criminal.

Some potentially useful land plants and animals are also rare or endangered. A few years ago, a young botany student in Mexico had been given a hot tip and found, after searching for some months, a plant that looked something like our cultivated corn (*Zea mays*), only it was taller and skinnier. Its name is *Zea diploperennis*. It is corn's closest relative and has several characteristics that make it phenomenally important to us. For one thing, it can cross-breed with corn, which no other native relatives of corn can do. For another, unlike our cultivated corn, it is a perennial. Every year farmers have to plow up the ground and plant new corn seed. But *Zea diploperennis* would need to be planted only once in every three or five or ten years. Because corn is the largest source of calories in many nations of Central America and Africa, and because corn production is worth billions of dollars in the United States, imagine the savings that would be possible if the genes for a perennial growth habit in corn could be obtained: the energy, money, and hours saved would be staggering.

Two other important features of *Zea diploperennis* are its ability to grow well in tropical climates, even in wet soils, and its resistance to a number of diseases. But the most arresting thing about this close relative of corn is that by all criteria that I can think of it is an endangered species. There are, or recently were, only about 3,000 of these plants in nature. They were discovered in Mexico in three tiny patches that were so small that a single bulldozer could have covered them over and caused the extinction of the species.

We must realize that there are undoubtedly many other such useful organisms living unnoticed that may be destroyed before we examine them and recognize their value. The majority of organisms on this planet, especially tropical species, have not yet been discovered and catalogued by scientists, let alone examined adequately for their potential value.

The worst enemies of insects are other insects. Many different species of parasitic insects do not bother people but parasitize other insects. What relevance does this have for our food supply? These insects and other organisms, such as viruses, fungi, bacteria, nematodes, and spiders, are essential for biological control of crop pests. For example, on the Eastern Shore of Maryland, the Mexican bean beetle is a serious pest of soybeans. A friend of mine, who is an entomology professor, found a little wasp from India that parasitizes the Mexican bean beetle. He developed a program for breeding the wasps in captivity and releasing them. The savings to farmers on the Eastern Shore may reach millions of dollars every year—this is the result of a very inexpensive biological control program.

INDUSTRIAL USES

Next we should look at species that are valuable as industrial raw materials. One of the reasons we are so rich in the United States today is because we have been so rich in trees. Trees have been the basis of our cheap construction. During millions of years, forests have produced fairly good soils, and now we are growing crops on them without rebuilding those soils. We are mining soil until it has been exhausted.

Forests also have provided us with paper. Paper is very important for civilization, and there are many places in the world where communication among people is inhibited by the simple lack of it. A plant originally found in East Africa, called kenaf, looks like marijuana, which sometimes causes problems. But kenaf (*Hibiscus cannabinus*), which belongs to the same genus as okra and other hibiscus plants, grows very quickly, 15 feet in a year, and its fibers make a fair quality of paper. It can be grown in areas where for one reason or another tree farming is not very practical. Also farmers do not have to wait long to get a return on their investment; in contrast, trees suitable for paper pulp are very slow-growing.

Now we turn to the deserts, which are apparent wastelands, useless and lifeless. I think most of us know that this is not true, but, nevertheless, many people look at these areas as being fundamentally unproductive and without economic value for human society, despite the interest and aesthetic values they have for us. Dr. Melvin Calvin of the University of California at Berkeley has been exploring the use of plants related to the poinsettia in the genus *Euphorbia*. These euphorbias grow in very arid areas. Instead of storing most of their energy as carbohydrates, they store it as hydrocarbons, a different kind of molecule. When these hydrocarbons are extracted from the plant and purified, the result is oil! The fluids from these euphorbias might well be substituted for several oil products, including diesel fuel, gasoline, or fuel oil. Of course, crude oil also once had its origins in the remains of living plants and animals that had soaked and baked under the earth for hundreds of millions of years. Euphorbias could possibly be grown as a crop in desert areas. We might find that the United States could offset some of its domestic petroleum use by cultivating these plants.

Dr. Eugenie Clark of the University of Maryland has found, to her astonishment, that sharks will pick one kind of Red Sea flounder up in their mouths and then spit it out. The flatfish produces a chemical that is a potent shark repellent, a product that has been sought for a longtime for the protection of swimmers. Similarly, squid have been found to produce an enzyme that breaks down certain nerve gases. Both the United States and the Soviet Union have stockpiled enormous amounts of nerve gases, but with suitable development perhaps the enzyme from squid could be used to dispose of some of the existing supplies. One must also wonder if such enzymes might be used to create effective defenses against the military use of nerve gases.

A somewhat more mundane waste-disposal problem is one created when cities deliver large amounts of human feces to the nation's waters. Usually, this material goes through sewage treatment plants, which take considerable energy to operate. A weedy plant, the water hyacinth from South America that chokes many waterways in the southern United States, has potential value because it grows very quickly and draws up large quantities of nutrients. For the water hyacinth, our wastes are nutrients! Not only that, but after suitable maceration and digestion with bacteria, this organism can be used to generate biogas fuel. This aquatic plant is an example of a living resource that should be investigated as a possible agent that may be used to change a problem into a benefit—in this case, a source of energy.

Let us now look at herbivores. I am specifically referring to those organisms that eat leaves of trees or fronds, and the leaf-like parts of algae, rather than to those that eat fruits or grains. Such herbivores have a problem: the material they eat is largely indigestable, or would be without the specialized microorganisms that live in the gut of a termite, the gut of a green sea turtle, or that once lived in the gut of a Steller's sea cow. If we can learn to cultivate these specialized microorganisms in the laboratory, we may be able to obtain methane and hydrogen or other kinds of gas from vegetable wastes. We can then burn these gases to keep our houses warm or to do our cooking. Thus, microorganisms as well as some plants could be used to recycle organic wastes into useful products, instead of being allowed to flow from their sources into oceans or fresh waters where they become a pollution problem.

M E D I C A L   U S E S

Lastly, we must look at the value of species for medicine. The tropical forests are perhaps the most endangered major class of ecosystem on the earth, together with their analogues, the tropical coral reefs. For reasons that we shall examine, tropical forests and tropical coral reefs are the best places to look for new medicines. Evolution has taken divergent paths in the cooler and warmer parts of the earth. In the cooler parts, the physical climate has been so demanding that organisms have evolved physiological and behavioral adaptations for coping with the weather. When winter comes, organisms can either dig a deep hole and go to sleep, develop an insulating layer of fur or feathers, or fly south. On the other hand, organisms living in the warmer parts of the earth, in tropical rainforests and coral reefs, have had to deal to a much greater extent with a different problem—one another. Because predation, parasitism, competition between species, and species-to-species interactions are all more intense in these warm places, the most common way in which species deal with one another is a way that Lucrezia Borgia would have been proud of—by poisoning.

Now what is poison? A poison is a chemical that in large amounts so disequilibrates the metabolism, the physiology of an organism, that it dies. Poisons in controlled use can have an opposite effect. Imagine, for example, a poison that would make the heart beat so fast that the heart muscle would quit from exhaustion, causing death. Such a poison in small, controlled doses could be beneficial for a person who has an abnormally slow heart beat. There also are poisons that kill by lowering blood pressure to the point where the cells do not get enough oxygen to have their wastes flushed away, so they die. Imagine using small amounts of these poisons for medicinal purposes in the treatment of high blood pressure.

Scientists are working on just such chemical agents today. Consider certain tropical sea cucumbers. Poke one of these animals, and it will do one of two things: it will regurgitate and turn its guts inside out or it will give forth a pinkish cloud in the water. That pinkish cloud is so poisonous that if you dropped a fish into the tide pool with the sea cucumber, the fish would turn belly-up in seconds. Interestingly, the percentage of poisonous species increases from the temperate zone to the tropics. This is true for many groups of organisms in addition to the sea cucumbers. These chemical deterrents to feeding are most frequently found in tropical organisms, on land or at sea, that have very limited motility and cannot swim, fly, or run away from their enemies. Sitting in one place with no defenses would leave them very vulnerable, so evolution favored them with chemicals that keep their enemies away.

The toxicity of mushrooms is legendary. I recently took a walk in the forests of Maryland with a world expert on mushrooms, and I was amazed by the number of mushrooms that even she could not identify. And this was Maryland! If we were in a little-known tropical area, such as Panama or Brazil, the chances that a mushroom would be known to science and its compounds adequately understood would be vanishingly small. However, the value to human beings of chemicals produced by mushrooms a year from now, or perhaps in tens or hundreds of years, might be enormous. We will never know if we cut down the tropical forests.

Many types of organisms produce toxic chemicals that have potential value for medical use. These include ferns, marine algae, many tropical sponges, and soft corals. Ferns, which grow in both the temperate zone and the tropics, are seldom eaten by phytophagous (plant-eating) insects because they contain chemical compounds that deter predation. Gorgonians, or soft corals, are one of the most interesting sources of compounds that have the potential for medicinal use. One species of gorgonian was such a rich source of the group of chemicals called prostaglandins that a drug company was thinking of using them directly as the source for a new generation of birth control agents. As it turns out, scientists do not necessarily have to harvest organisms continuously from the wild to obtain useful compounds. Synthetic variants of the compounds can be developed from many species that are taken into the laboratory. But these substances could not be identified and synthesized without a model, the basic template provided by the living organism. This is what is now being done in the case of prostaglandins.

Just a couple of years ago, scientists found that a species of nudibranch, a shell-less marine snail, produces a very powerful hypotensive agent. A small amount of it drastically lowers the blood pressure of experimental animals in the laboratory. Imagine how people around the world who suffer or die of high blood pressure and strokes each year would profit if we could develop prescription drugs from organisms such as these! Puffer fishes, or Fugu fishes, contain a powerful poison called tetrodotoxin that has a profound effect on the conduction of nerve impulses. This chemical is a fundamentally important tool for basic scientific inquiry into the workings of nerves.

Horseshoe crabs also have medicinal value. The cells in the blood of a horseshoe crab react extremely readily and observably to the presence of certain kinds of toxins from bacteria. Formerly, persons receiving intraveneous injections sometimes received fluids contaminated by exceedingly tiny amounts of toxins from bacteria. Severe allergic reactions to these undetected toxins could cause death. The blood cells of the horseshoe crab are a hundred times more sensitive in detecting bacterial endotoxins than are the blood cells from rabbits, which were previously used to detect these toxins. They are also much cheaper.

A final example is the embryo of the sea urchin, which undergoes a development much like that of the human embryo. As we have introduced into our environment a large number of novel compounds—polychlorinated biphenyls, DDT, and so on—the sea urchin embryo has become invaluable in screening the chemicals to see just what effects they may have on the development of an individual. Where would we be without these organisms for such tests? I think we would be in even worse shape than we are now.

Conserving biological diversity is the issue. Can we afford, knowing what we now know and knowing how much we still have to learn, to let species become extinct when we can see so many sound reasons for preserving them? I think not. Besides those that provide us with clean water and valuable medicines, there are many creatures, from fruit flies to great apes, that can provide us with profound insights into our own species. When we endanger many of these species, what next will we be endangering?

6

The Realities Of Preserving Species In Captivity

ULYSSES S. SEAL

Time and events have forced us to realize and respond to the fact that, for a large segment of the life forms of this planet, evolution by natural selection has ceased. The best we can do for these species is to preserve options for the next generation. We must develop strategies for management that preserve for our descendents choices to reestablish natural populations. Such strategies must include multiple options because any one strategy may not be successful.

My goal in this presentation is to describe a bit of the science that is being developed as the basis for captive-breeding programs. I include not just the breeding programs in zoos but also those needed in most of the parks and reserves of the world.

Dr. Myers described the impending spasm of extinctions as a challenge. I suggest that to face that challenge we must become aware of another challenge. Virtually all the reserves and game parks of the world are no more satisfactory for long-term survival of large species than are zoological parks; they are too small. Their small area, relative to the needs for viable populations of large mammals, birds, and trees, requires application of new management principles. These principles are based upon concepts appropriate to small populations distributed in fragmented patches of habitat or living space—not only in zoos but also in parks and reserves.

CONSERVATION AND PRESERVATION

Ecologists speak about efforts to conserve and maintain natural eco-systems, those biological communities in which there is a potential for evolution by natural selection on a continuing basis.

The distinction between "conservation" and "preservation" is important. By preservation we refer to the effort to maintain, in managed breeding circumstances ranging from reserves to zoos, a large enough population of a particular species to ensure its survival while also retaining enough genetic variability in the original population so that future adaptations may be possible. Under these managed conditions, we would attempt to avoid artificial or human-imposed selection and would recognize that the processes of natural selection would be relaxed. Our goal for conservation would be to return animals to a free-ranging habitat under circumstances that allow evolution by natural selection and accumulation of new variation by mutation at a rate faster than the loss by genetic drift.

It ordinarily is not possible to maintain a sufficiently large population of the large, long-lived, slowly reproducing species under captive circumstances or in most reserves or parks for these species to continue to evolve by natural selection. Most of our current "conservation" programs for these large species of animals and plants are at best preservation programs. Captive-preservation programs involving these species simply try to reduce the loss of genetic variability by drift and inbreeding, thereby making future conservation possible.

We believe that plans for preserving endangered species must be formulated in terms of returning captive-bred individuals to the wild under conditions as close as possible to those under which the species originally evolved and will continue to evolve by natural selection. This is the guiding principle in the formulation of the concepts presented here.

TIME AND CONSERVATION

The crucial question for our planning is time. How long do we have to plan for? As human beings, we divide magnitudes of time that are too great for us to deal with into daily and weekly events: the calendar, school, or tax year; and life history landmarks such as birth, school graduation, marriage, first job, and perhaps retirement. Therefore, when we talk about maintaining a species for a hundred or a thousand years, people look aghast and tend to think we may be idiots who do not have any concept of the real world. But there is not just one "reality." There are many realities, and each of us may select a different one.

The facet of reality most damaging for zoos today emanates from a business school environment. It is the notion that the time span for measuring success—the success or failure of any project—is about three months to one year. Successful performance must be almost instantly apparent.

What is the time span of concern for preservation of species? The data that we have from population genetics suggest we have to plan at a minimum for 100 to 200 years, and, in a very real sense, in managing breeding it is economic to plan for 1,000 years or longer. If we do not, options for the survival of these species will greatly diminish within less than 100 years. We are talking about species with generation times ranging from one to ten years, on the average. Thus, we need to plan in the short-term to use strategies that will allow these species to survive in a preservation mode for hundreds of years. This may provide the time necessary to re-establish a complex network of interrelated ecosystems that, in the future, will permit conservation of species in the wild.

Some suggest that within 20 years a miracle will occur on earth and a decision made to change the entire strategy by which we human beings live with our planet. If we do not plan far ahead, the options we still have can drift away from us within the 20 to 100 years during which we hope change will occur. We want to preserve options, and that means following a "safe-to-fail" strategy—not a "fail-safe" one. We must provide a margin for repeated failure.

COMPONENTS OF A PRESERVATION STRATEGY

Some questions to ask in developing a captive-breeding strategy include: (1) what is the capacity of zoos, (2) how do we choose species for captive-breeding programs, (3) how many initial individuals or founders are necessary to represent adequately the population or species, (4) what population size must we maintain for a species, (5) how will we manage the breeding (genetics) and demography (age and sex structure) of the captive population, (6) under what circumstances will exchange between wild and captive populations or return of captives to free-ranging populations occur, and (7) when can an organized captive preservation or propagation program be terminated?

Zoo Capacity

About 150 zoos are engaged in breeding programs in North America. They occupy nearly 90 square kilometers (35 square miles). This area is being asked to provide a captive species propagation and preservation resource for 300 to 400 endangered species, and perhaps as many as 1,000 species, in the next two decades. The total annual budget for operating these zoos is about $250 million. Bear in mind that none of these budgets is allocated specifically for species preservation. Zoos have been established primarily as recreational institutions and are only secondarily developing programs in conservation, education, and research.

The total number of nonfish vertebrate animals currently housed in these North American zoos is about 150,000 specimens. The total number of species is about 4,000. If we consider just the mammals, there are approximately 50,000 mammalian specimens currently in these zoos, representing 800 to 1,000 species. So there are, on average, 50 animals of each mammalian species distributed over these 150 zoos. Overall attendance per year is over 100 million people, so a substantial percentage of the population is able to see this range of species—all to the good! These figures give us a first approximation of current zoo capacities in North America.

What kinds of mammals are there in zoos? Species occurring in zoos do not accurately reflect the proportions of living mammalian species in the wild. For instance, there is a tremendous underrepresentation in zoos of some animal groups such as bats, which represent around 20 percent of living mammalian species but less than 1 percent of species held in zoos. The ungulates, the Artiodactyla and the Perissodactyla, constitute about 40 percent of zoo-held animals, a vast majority of these being artiodactyls. Primates constitute 24 percent and carnivores 18 percent. Zoos are highly selective for these species because they are visible and more easily enjoyed by zoo visitors. All other mammals, including bats, make up the remaining 18 percent.

Frequently, ungulates, primates, and carnivores are also keystone species: those that influence the species composition of their ecosystems to a greater extent than predicted by their numbers alone. However, we must remember that a captive-propagation program takes a species out of its ecosystem and preserves it as an isolated population of animals. The odds are almost 100 percent that the ecosystem to which a species is returned will not be identical to the biological community from which it was taken. A new set of relationships will be established upon insertion of a species into a geographic area from which it has been absent or has never occupied. We cannot recapture the past, and our skills in predicting the future are modest. What we are doing in each preservation program holds no certain guarantee of success, and zoo professionals have few illusions about that.

Choice of Species

We know that multicellular species on earth number in the millions. I am going to consider primarily some 20,000 to 25,000 species—that is, the nonfish vertebrates. Fish vertebrates would add another 30,000 species and different management problems, but the principles here will apply to a much wider range of species. In any event, the current locations of zoos and their programs lead them to focus primarily on the nonfish vertebrates.

Ecologists often point to the difficulty in choosing the appropriate individual animals or plants to be representative of the species selected for captive-breeding programs. This difficulty arises because of the continuing selection and adaptation that occur in each population as a result of long-term interaction with particular environments. Matching environments simply cannot be provided in captivity and cannot be predicted for the future. We will need to preserve the maximum amount of diversity to allow for selection in the inevitably new and changed environments of the future. None will be "natural" in the sense of being untouched by man or unchanged by time.

What is the magnitude of the species selection problem? The need is to preserve as many species as possible. Fortunately, we do not have to choose from among a million species that fit the limits of our particular goals and capabilities. How do we choose these species? We are currently using three major sets of criteria. The key criterion is endangerment in the wild. To establish the status of a species and its habitats requires surveys of wild populations, especially those in areas of increasing human activity. This information is compiled in the International Union for the Conservation of Nature and Natural Resources (IUCN) Red Data Books. Second, we must consider if the species can be managed in captivity with existing and anticipated resources. Third, the taxonomic level must be considered. Many of our choices have been at the species and subspecies level. People, in general, are fascinated by differences within species and love to recognize them formally. For example, we are faced with at least four different varieties of tigers that are listed as endangered. Eighty-two varieties or subspecies are identified for the eight large felids maintained in institutions participating in the International Species Inventory System (ISIS) (Table 1). If our global objective is the maintenance of the widest range of genetic diversity possible, then we will not be able to preserve by captive propagation every named subspecies, race, or population of each species. Our capacity is limited.

These are the problems of choosing species, or of "playing God" and building the ark. Our zoos, parks, and reserves are the ark, or the lifeboat, on which these species are to be floated.

Size and Expansion of Founder Populations

If we are given the choice, how many individuals of a species should we take from a wild population for a captive-breeding program to represent the genetic diversity or additive genetic variance of that species? If I am asked to establish a captive program, should I use one pregnant female, hopefully with a male offspring, or do I need two, ten, a hundred or a thousand individuals? What age should they be? How many of each sex should be included? How much of the genetic diversity of a species does one creature carry? It is interesting that in the Biblical story of Noah, the animals marched aboard at a minimum of "six-by-six," and not the familiar "two-by-two." We will see that this number, three pairs of each species, has a sound scientific basis because it retains a substantial amount of genetic diversity.

The genetic diversity or heterozygosity (H) that a group of founding individuals carries can be readily calculated with a pocket calculator from the following equation:

$$\text{Effects on heterozygosity: } H = 1 - \frac{1}{2N_e} \qquad \text{(Equation 1)}$$

Heterozygosity (H) equals one minus one divided by $2N_e$, where N_e is equal to the effective population size or the approximate number of reproducing animals. Using this equation, we find that heterozygosity increases from .50 to .99 as we increase the population size from 1 to 50 individuals. In other words, 1 individual represents approximately 50 percent of the genetic diversity, 2 individuals represent 75 percent, and 10

Table I Capacity of captive facilities for preserving large felids.*

Species	Living subspecies	Endangered subspecies[†]	Facilities maintaining species	Population	Potential subspecies for population size[#]		
					100	250	500
Tiger (Panthera tigris)	8	8	110	450	4	2	1
Lion (Panthera leo)	11	1	97	381	4	1	1
Leopard (Panthera pardus)	15	15	72	246	2	1	0
Jaguar (Panthera onca)	8	8	65	178	2	1	0
Puma (Felis concolor)	29	2	69	173	2	1	0
Cheetah (Acinonyx jubatus)	6	6	32	166	2	1	0
Snow leopard (Panthera uncia)	1	1	35	128	1	1	0
Clouded leopard (Neofelis nebulosa)	4	4	20	63	1	0	0
Totals	82	45	—	1,785	18	7	4

*Information compiled for facilities that participate in the International Species Inventory System (ISIS). ISIS facilities include most American zoos and some foreign facilities. (Modified from Foose 1983.)

[†] From listings in the International Union for the Conservation of Nature and Natural Resources, Red Data Book (IUCN, 1966, et. seq.)

[#] Population sizes represent three theoretical levels of self-sustaining breeding populations, or those large enough to avoid significant inbreeding. Column totals may differ from calculated totals, which represent approximate capacity of facilities rather than existing breeding stock of specific subspecies.

Table 2   *Genetic diversity in a small population sample.*

N	H
1	.50
2	.75
6	.92
10	.95
50	.99

individuals 95 percent. Notice that we approach an asymptote with 6 individuals at 92 percent (Table 2).

Thus, the biblical choice of six animals, or three pairs, was indeed a wise absolute minimum choice if we assume that all survived and reproduced. From these calculations, we can immediately draw a major conclusion: As few as ten individuals capable of reproducing can provide us with a substantial sample of the additive genetic variance of a species, particularly if five pairs are involved. The sex ratio needs to be equal.

A population loses heterozygosity from one generation (t) to the next in relation to its size.

$$\text{Effects on heterozygosity: } H = \left(1 - \frac{1}{2N_e}\right)^t \qquad \text{(Equation 2)}$$

If we expand the expression for each generation, additional loss of heterozygosity occurs (Table 3). This teaches us a very important lesson: If we are going to maintain a species in captivity and retain the genetic diversity of the founders, it is important that we expand that population, beginning with our six or ten breeding animals, to our maximum carrying capacity as rapidly as possible.

Table 3 illustrates this lesson. If we expand our population to 100 individuals, then after 10 generations the population will lose only 5 percent of its heterozygosity or genetic variability, whereas a population beginning with 10 animals will lose 40 percent. This is why the size of the population that we are capable of maintaining over time and the speed with which we achieve that size are very important.

Table 3 *How fast is genetic variability lost?*

N_e	Generation (t)		
	1	5	10
10	.95	.77	.60
30	.98	.92	.85
50	.99	.95	.90
100	.995	.975	.95

A famous case that gives us a perspective on captive breeding and is useful in illustrating many of these relationships is the Przewalski horse or *Equus przewalskii* (Figure 1). Przewalski horses have disappeared in the wild, become extinct, within the past four decades. There are no Przewalski horses wild in Mongolia, and it is unlikely that they will be returned successfully to that habitat in the near future.

Fifty-three of these animals were brought into captivity over a period of 20 or 30 years in the early part of the century. A total of just 17 of those 53 animals served as founders for all the current living stock, around 400 to 500 animals. Actually, 11 or 12 wild horses plus a domestic mare contributed most of the founder genes. Inbreeding occurred as early as 1912, reached a plateau in the 1930s, and then started to increase again in the 1970s. This inbreeding occurred at a much more rapid rate than was necessary on the basis of the number of founder animals that originally were available. The result has been an unnecessary loss of genetic diversity.

The captive-breeding history of Siberian tigers over six generations provides another well-documented illustration of these concepts (Figure 2). Records show that 68 animals were brought into captivity from the Siberian population. Of the current population of 1,014, only 26 in Russian zoos and 3 in East Germany are wild-born. Thus, more than 97 percent of the world's zoo population is captive bred. However, only 6 animals have provided 69.4 percent of the founder contribution to the living captive bred population (Figure 3). Another 6 animals contributed 18.9 percent and 32 other tigers, 11.7 percent. Records on the captive population between 1957 and the present show that inbred litters were first produced in 1965. The mean level of inbreeding has continued at a moderate level (around 0.12) since that time. There has not been effective usage of most of the wild-caught stock to either minimize inbreeding or to preserve the genetic diversity available in these animals.

Figure 1 *Przewalski's horse (Equus przewalskii),* a species now thought to be extinct in the wild. Illustration by Sally Bensusen.

A N I M A L

Management and Determinants of Effective Population Size

It is important to recognize that inbreeding is undesirable, and that it can be avoided in managing captive species. Inbreeding either by father and daughter crosses or brother and sister crosses results in decreased neonatal survival and reduced fecundity in many species for which pedigree histories are available from zoo records (Ralls and Ballou 1983). Inbreeding causes shorter life spans in Siberian tigers (Seal and Foose 1983). About 19 of 20 species for which data are available exhibited deleterious effects of inbreeding. It is highly likely that similar effects would result from inbreeding in small wild populations as well.

Two breeding strategies are available for avoiding inbreeding in the management of our captive populations. Both of them relate to a notion called "effective population size," a key genetic concept for managing captive species. You will hear this term repeatedly during the coming years in discussions of the management of small populations. We are using this concept as the basis for our analysis of captive-breeding programs planned in the zoo world. It is also beginning to be applied to an evaluation of small wild populations. In this method, evaluation of the effective population size and its relationship to the rate of loss of heterozygosity is accomplished by analysis of the breeding strategy over two to three generations.

There are three determinants of effective population size (N_e), and therefore the amount of inbreeding. They are: (1) the sex ratio in the breeding population, (2) the variation in family size or representation of parents in the next generation, and (3) the size of the population. These effects can be calculated for a constant, nongrowing population using the following equations that have been simplified from Crow and Kimura (1970):

The effect of the sex ratio on $N_e = \dfrac{4 \times M \times F}{N}$ (Equation 3)

The effect of the variance of family size on $N_e = \dfrac{4N - 2}{V_k + 2}$ (Equation 4)

or approximately $N_e = \dfrac{4N}{V_k + 2}$

Where: N = number of breeding males and females,
        M = number of breeding males,

Figure 2 *The Siberian tiger (Panthera tigris tigris) is an endangered species in the wild. Illustration by Vichai Malikul.*

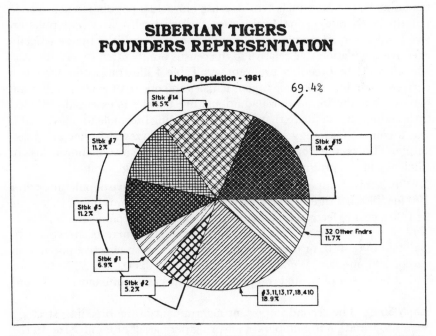

Figure 3   Representation of founders in living Siberian tiger populations (1981). Studbook numbers (STBK) are given to identify individual founders. The 69.4 percent figure indicates the share of offspring produced by six major founders.

F = number of breeding females, and
V_k = variance in family size per parent.

(See Crow and Kimura 1970 for calculating the variance of family size.)

Sex Ratio. The importance of sex ratios is illustrated in Table 4. If we have five males and five females in our beginning breeding population of ten animals, the N_e equals ten. Because our actual population size also is ten, the N_e/N ratio is one. In this case, the genetically effective population size is about equal to our actual population size, and it is the genetically effective population size relative to the census number that determines the efficiency of our breeding program. As Table 4 illustrates, the difference between breeding one male to four females and one to nine is such that the genetic contribution of those additional five females is essentially wasted by breeding them only to that one stud. Breeding one male to nine females was a common strategy in the breeding of the Przewalski horse, for example. This resulted in a much lower sex ratio and a tremendous loss of efficiency in the program of genetic and animal management.

Why is this? Suppose we wish to manage for an effective population size of 100 for Siberian tigers, and we know that each of them is going to cost us $1,000 a year to feed and maintain, a total of $100,000 per year if $N_e/N=1$. Now if we use a less-efficient breeding strategy, it may be necessary to maintain 300, 400, or even 500 tigers to achieve that effective population size of 100 animals. We are then talking about $200,000, $300,000, or $400,000 a year of wasted resources in our species maintenance program!

Family Size. The second important determinant in the breeding strategy relates to variation in numbers of offspring per parent or family size. In the captive history of the Przewalski horse and of the Siberian tiger, there has

Table 4   *Sex ratios—how many males?*

Males	Females	N_e	N_e/N (for N = 10)
5	5	10	1
1	9	3.6	.36
2	8	6.4	.64
1	4	3.2	.64

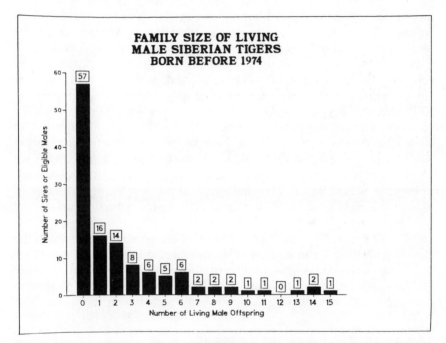

Figure 4   *Male offspring sired by male Siberian tigers. This measure of family size illustrates the large variation in births between families up to 1974.*

been enormous variation in family size. Some stallions sired 36 offspring, some 20, and a very large number of males had no offspring. A similar pattern has occurred with the tigers (Figure 4). The animals that were not bred made no genetic contribution to the next generation. They were totally wasted in the maintenance program. They might as well not have been maintained. This has also been true for the female Przewalski horses and Siberian tigers. A large number of females never entered the breeding pool. These were animals that survived to breeding age and should have had the opportunity to breed but did not. Again there was a tremendous wastage. These disparate family sizes and frequent backcrosses of daughters to sires are also the basis for the increase in inbreeding coefficients.

For maximum efficiency in maintaining a captive population and in achieving the highest possible effective population size, we wish *each* parent to contribute the *same number* of offspring to the next generation. With that strategy, family-size variation becomes zero. The equation for variance in family size given at the beginning of this section (Equation 4) shows that the effective population size is larger than the actual population when there is no variation in family size between parents. For example, we obtain an effective population size of 20 for a census population of 10 and, in effect, a ratio of 2 to 1. This mathematical relationship provides a yield of almost 2 effective animals for each of our original census animals.

Stability of Effective Population Size. The third important determinant in the breeding strategy is the stability of the numbers of breeding animals. Figure 5 shows the rates of loss of diversity over generations as a function of effective population size (Equation 2). The x-axis is numbers of generations up to 50, and loss of genetic diversity is shown on the y-axis. The

Table 5 *Variation in family size is expensive.*

V_k	N	N_e	$\dfrac{N_e}{N}$
0	10	20	2.0
1	10	13.3	1.3
2	10	10*	1.0
4	10	6.7	0.67

*Note: By equalizing family size, we can maintain more genetic diversity (a higher N_e) than by just equalizing sex ratios because the ratio $N_e/N=2$ when the family size is equal ($V_k=0$), while $N_e/N=1$ when the sex ratio is equal.

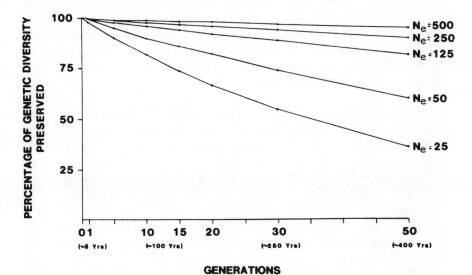

Figure 5   Decline of genetic diversity over 50 generations for various effective population sizes (N_e). Calculations are based on the maintenance of a stable population (N) of 250 animals. (Figure derived from Foose 1983.)

rate of loss is a very dramatic function of effective population size. At 50 generations and with an effective population size of 8, about 80 percent is lost, whereas with an effective population size of 125 at 50 generations, 80 percent is retained. It is possible to get an effective population size of 125 with as few as 65 individuals if the breeding strategy is optimal. This suggests that with an actual population size of 125 animals, the population could do quite well for a short period of time—say 50 generations. I suggest, however, that we must think in terms of much longer periods.

Now if the population sizes are allowed to oscillate—200 one generation and 20 the next—then we lose these advantages. The amount of heterozygosity retained, depending upon the character of the swings, is a harmonic mean of the peaks and valleys, not simply the arithmetic mean or average. We are far better off to choose conditions that allow us to maintain a stable effective population size.

Target Minimum Population Size. Currently available information indicates that the minimum effective population size necessary to retain all of the genetic diversity of vertebrates in captivity is about 250 to 500. We may take 250 as a lower limit. This would allow us to preserve a species under such circumstances that the rate of gain of new variation might approximately equal the rate of loss of variation by drift over a long period of time. If zoos or reserve managers are going to take a genuinely long-term view in any captive management plan, they must consider these numbers. In fact, the numbers may need to be higher depending on the breeding strategy used.

Consider the example of tigers: among the tiger reserves in the world, few are self-sustaining from this point of view. One large managed tiger reserve is the Chitawan National Forest in Nepal. It supports a total breeding population of about 30 adult tigers. It is not likely that their N_e is 60; it may be 30 but is probably closer to 15. Therefore, the likelihood of the tigers in that population going extinct is high. They will lose genetic variability by drift, and selection will have little or no effect on the outcome.

We can now see why a breeding strategy that pays close attention to sex ratios and family size will achieve a desired maximum effective population size much more economically than a random or local option strategy. This allows us to use our resources far more efficiently. Instead of being able to maintain only 100 species of nonfish vertebrates in captivity in an effective manner, we can possibly maintain as many as 500 vertebrate species with current resources—if we so choose. Our options change very dramatically when we pay attention to some fundamental rules of population and evolutionary biology.

Exchange and Return of Animals to Wild Populations

Zoos working in the Species Survival Plan (SSP) program are trying to manage captive populations with the objective of returning representatives to protected wild habitats. We also foresee, with tigers and other species such as the rhinoceros, that ultimately there will be a genetic exchange between small wild populations and captive populations. This will be necessary because the problems of small, effective population size and the need for a supportive captive gene pool to allow these species to survive make this interaction inevitable. The strategy and mechanisms for these exchanges have not been thoroughly formulated and tested.

Technology is one area under investigation for ensuring and facilitating breeding. More than 200 efforts to artificially inseminate big cats have been made, with 2 successes. It would be a tremendous boost to genetic management if success could be achieved with artificial insemination and related technologies such as embryo transfer and cryostorage of embryos. A significant amount of effort on the big cats has been made by a number of groups, but it has not been successful. We need to learn much more about the female reproductive cycle of wild felids. Ultimately, we would like to achieve long-term sperm, ovum, and embryo storage. It would be far simpler to transfer the sperm of the rhinoceros from one zoo to another than to transfer the animal itself for breeding.

Resources Required

I suggested in the case of tigers that perhaps 250 was a minimum effective population size for preserving captive, self-sustaining populations on a sufficiently long-term basis to be of merit. This, in turn, suggests that if we converted all of our zoo resources to nothing but endangered species we might maintain perhaps 500 species, depending upon their trophic distribution. It is obvious that a thousand whales are dramatically different from a thousand tree shrews. Consideration must be given to available resources.

Human resources are a major need. I have been working on the Siberian tiger now for five years. It requires a substantial number of hours each week to contribute to the management of the North American SSP Program. We need more knowledgeable people who can spend the great amount of time that is required. Zoos do not have enough people allocated to the task. They are having a difficult time establishing 40 programs, let alone the 500 that are needed. Each zoo will, on the average, need to pro-

vide three to five species coordinators and participate in perhaps fifty programs. Participation means following a plan and guidelines for a breeding
program and distribution of animals. Funds are limited. This limitation
may have a greater effect on the species selection process than will space or
animal availability.

Current Programs

International Studbooks.   International Studbooks were the first efforts to
partially coordinate managed breeding programs through detailed record-
keeping of pedigrees and census information. Several were started many
decades ago and were the result of the interest and effort of dedicated individuals. There are now 56 studbooks, of which 48 are active (Table 6).
They serve as a focus for international cooperation, and their numbers are
beginning to increase with the advent of regional breeding programs. The
studbooks are supported and endorsed by the International Union for Directors of Zoological Gardens and are coordinated by the staff of the International Zoo Yearbook, located at the London Zoological Society. The
International Tiger Studbook is worldwide in coverage and updates are
distributed yearly. It is incredibly detailed, and Dr. Siegfried Seifert, director of the Leipzig Zoo, has done a Herculean job with this volume.

International Species Inventory System (ISIS).   ISIS, a computerized captive
animal data file, and the Species Survival Plan (SSP) program illustrate
the scope of zoo activities necessary for sustained captive management of
species. Zoos are currently spending more than $100,000 a year on ISIS, a
program begun in 1974. Since then, a steady growth in the number of
participants has occurred. The program includes 175 participants, including more than a dozen zoos in Europe, and has gained sufficient momen-
tum to provide the basis for a worldwide cooperative effort. It is possible
that an effective international cooperative program will enhance the overall
captive-carrying capacity and increase the number of species that can be
managed in captivity as genetically and demographically viable populations. Similar efforts are being explored in the Southern Hemisphere
as well.

How many living mammals are listed in the ISIS inventory? Some
32,000. Birds were added to the program in 1979, and now about 20,000
specimens are listed. The inclusion of reptiles and amphibians will be
made soon. A significant fraction of the mammals that are in North Ameri-

Table 6   *Species with international studbooks.*

Reptiles	Chinese alligator	
Birds	Kiwi	Red-cheeked ibis
	Cabot's tragopan	Edward's pheasant
	White-eared pheasant	Red-crowned crane
	White-naped crane	Bali mynah
Mammals		
Marsupial	Brush-tailed bettong	
Primates	Black lemur	Ruffed lemur
	Pygmy marmoset	Golden lion tamarin
	Lion-tailed macaque	Douc langur
	Orangutan	Gorilla
	Bonobo or Pygmy chimpanzee	
Edentate	Giant anteater	
Rodent	Pacarana	
Carnivores	Red wolf	Mexican wolf
	Bush dog	Maned wolf
	Polar bear	Spectacled bear
	Giant panda	Red panda
	Asiatic lion	Brown hyaena
	Rare tigers	Clouded leopard
	Snow leopard	Rare leopards
Ungulates	Przewalski horse	Asiatic wild ass
	African wild ass	Grevy's zebra
	Indian rhinoceros	Black rhinoceros
	White rhinoceros	Pygmy hippopotamus
	Vicuna	Eld's deer
	Pere David's deer	Pudu
	Pampas deer	Okapi
	Gaur	European bison
	Wood bison	Lechwe waterbuck
	Arabian oryx	Slender-horned gazelle
	Japanese serow	

can collections are already in the inventory, and they are being followed in terms of census, pedigrees, and demographic data. The ISIS office processes around 100,000 forms a year. This is a large workload, but it composes the data base on which zoo breeding plans, species survival plans, and a number of other analyses now depend.

Species Survival Program. The American Association of Zoological Parks and Aquariums (AAZPA) has established several Species Survival Plans in North America (Table 7). Each of these plans has a species coordinator and is similar to the tiger program I mentioned earlier. Each plan is being developed to cope with the problems we have described. In order to manage animals as a single population, cooperation between the several institutions that own and house the species is essential. In the case of tigers, I work with 50 different institutions in North America alone. The institutions complete a memorandum of agreement and do not give up ownership. All cooperation is voluntary in the most fundamental sense. We request agreement on goals and agreement to follow the same guidelines for genetic and population management.

It is ironic that when these captive-breeding programs are successful, the economic value of a species may decline to nearly zero. The success of

Table 7   Species designated for AAZPA species survival plans.

Reptiles	Chinese alligator	Radiated tortoise
	Aruba Island rattlesnake	Indian python
	Madagascan ground boa	
Birds	Bali mynah	White-naped crane
	Andean condor	Humboldt's penguin
Mammals	Ruffed lemur	Black lemur
	Golden lion tamarin	Lion-tailed macaque
	Gorilla	Orangutan
	Siberian tiger	Asian small-clawed otter
	Asian lion	Snow leopard
	Cheetah	Chacoan peccary
	Indian rhino	Black rhino
	Sumatran rhino	White rhino
	Asiatic wild horse	Grevy's zebra
	Barasingha	Okapi
	Gaur	Arabian oryx
	Scimitar-horned oryx	

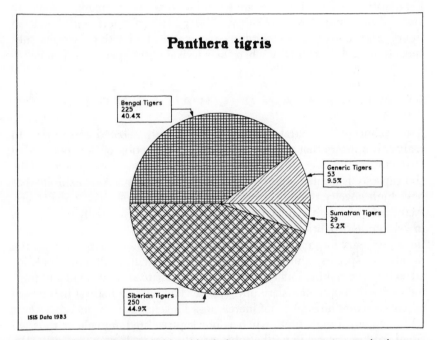

Figure 6   *Kinds of tigers held in North American zoos reporting to the International Species Inventory System (ISIS) in 1983. Generic tigers have been bred without regard to geographical differences between races or forms.*

reproduction is illustrated by the demographic calculation of the consequences of allowing female tigers in the current population to have one
litter every other year while maintaining current mortality rates—within
20 years we could have 6,000 tigers! We are obviously not going to do
this, but the tremendous breeding potential is a significant problem. The
reproduction program for the Siberian tiger has been so successful that we
now make wide use of implanted contraceptives to help limit reproduction. Another limitation is zoo-carrying capacity, which brings us back to
the question of species choice: are we going to be able to maintain separate
viable captive populations of Siberian tigers, Bengal tigers, and Sumatran
tigers (Figure 6)? Can we afford to concern ourselves with preserving subspecies or races in captivity when the survival of the species is at stake?

SUMMARY AND CHALLENGES

These concepts and strategies are being actively debated and tested. In
reality, it appears that we can preserve only a fraction of the endangered
forms by captive-breeding programs, and that we must make choices. Our
zoo capacity is limited, and there is competition for space by exhibits that
have high novelty value to attract the viewing public such as white tigers.
Acquiring founders may be difficult and expensive, especially for animals
in remote and politically unstable areas. The size of the captive populations necessary for genetic survival means that zoos will have to reduce the
number of species exhibited. This is in conflict with traditional goals for
attracting the public. Difficult problems on how to sustain small and fragmented wild populations are unresolved. The wild or natural habitats of
species are diminishing—not increasing. The character of the ecosystems
will change through time, whereas our captive-bred animals or those in
small wild reserves will not be subject to the same selective pressures. We
must preserve as much genetic diversity as possible to provide the material
for selection when animals are returned to these changed systems.

Strategy is a basic issue. I would seek a safe-to-fail strategy: a set of options for the maintenance of a species that will allow for a number of failures and catastrophes. When captive-bred animals are returned to wild
habitats, we must anticipate that the reintroductions or the restocking
plans or the management programs may fail 10 percent of the time, or they
may fail 50 percent of the time, or they may even fail 90 percent of the
time. Knowing this, we need to preserve options to allow for these trials
and failures in the future.

This is our captive-breeding ethic.

References Cited and Additional Readings

Barney, G. O.
1980. The Global 2000 Report to the President—Entering the Twenty-First Century, Vol. II, The Technical Report. Washington, D.C.: U.S. Government Printing Office.

Crow, J. F. and M. Kimura.
1970. *An Introduction to Population Genetics Theory.* Minneapolis: Burgess Publishing Co.

Foose, T. J.
1983. The relevance of captive populations to the conservation of biotic diversity. In *Genetics and Conservation: A Reference for Managing Wild Animal and Plant Populations*, ed. C. M. Schonewald-Cox, S. M. Chambers, B. MacBryde, and W. L. Thomas. Menlo Park, Calif.: Benjamin-Cummings Publishing Co., 374–401.

Frankel, O. H. and M. E. Soule.
1981. *Conservation and Evolution.* Cambridge: Cambridge University Press.

IUCN (International Union for the Conservation of Nature and Natural Resources).
1966. 1966 et seq. Red Data Book, Volume 1. *Mammals.* IUCN, Morges, Switzerland (loose-leaf).

Ralls, K. and J. Ballou.
1983. Extinction: lessons from zoos. In *Genetics and Conservation: A Reference for Managing Wild Amimal and Plant Populations*, ed. C. M. Schonewald-Cox, S. M. Chambers, B. MacBryde, and W. L. Thomas. Menlo Park, Calif.: Benjamin-Cummings Publishing Co. 164–84.

Schonewald-Cox, C. M., S. M. Chambers, B. MacBryde, and W. L. Thomas, eds.
1983. *Genetics and Conservation: A Reference for Managing Wild Animal and Plant Populations.* Menlo Park, Calif.: Benjamin-Cummings Publishing Co.

Seal, U. S. and T. J. Foose.
1983. Development of a master plan for captive propagation of Siberian tigers in North American zoos. *Zoo Biology* 2:241–44.

Soule, M. E. and B. A. Wilcox, eds.
1980. *Conservation Biology: An Evolutionary-Ecological Perspective.* Sunderland, Mass.: Sinauer Associates.

7

Strategies For Preserving Species In The Wild

THOMAS E. LOVEJOY

There is more than one way to approach a discussion of strategies for conserving plant and animal life. There are scientific strategies, which I will concentrate on in this presentation, and there are also political strategies for effectively "marketing" conservation by reaching out and convincing the public of its importance. Another strategy that has become more widely known in the last few years is the "World Conservation Strategy" (International Union for the Conservation of Nature and Natural Resources 1980), which is an attempt to articulate more clearly than heretofore the relationships between conservation and development and between conservation and human welfare.

In this discussion, I will focus on the tropical areas of the world, particularly the tropical forests. Conservationists who have an international responsibility are particularly concerned with tropical forests (which girdle the globe at the equator wherever there is sufficient rainfall) because they hold an enormous number of species (Figure 1). Something like half of all the species of plant and animal life on this planet occur in these tropical forests. These forests are teeming with species, and they make a biologist almost dizzy the first time he or she visits one.

I will concentrate on the Amazon because it is the tropical forest with which I am most familiar. This great forest, the largest remaining one, occupies a huge drainage basin in South America. This forest alone is most conservatively estimated to hold 10 percent of all the species of plant and animal life on this planet. To get an idea of the variety, compare a temperate forest in southern New England, where one finds ten or twenty species

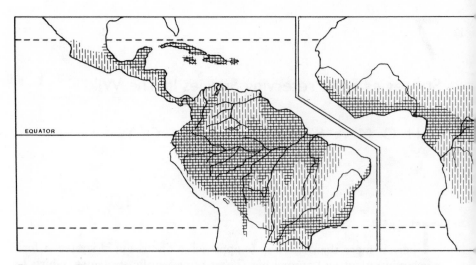

Figure I   *Tropical forests of the world. Evergreen rainforests and semideciduous forests are two major types of tropical forests. Illustration by Kathleen Spagnola, adapted from Grzimek 1974.*

of trees in the entire forest community, with a tropical forest in Amazonian Peru, where about 300 species of trees are found in an area of just 10 hectares, roughly 25 acres. The individuals of a species are often widely scattered, and it is frequently difficult to find a second individual of the same species. This pattern is repeated in group after group of organisms. A curious exception is the bumblebee (*Bombus*), represented by only one species in the entire Amazon Basin.

Huge areas of tropical forest in the Amazon are rapidly being cleared, and the same thing is happening to tropical forests in the Old World, in Africa and in Asia. Every time even a small area, a square kilometer, is cleared off for grazing or agriculture, millions of organisms are done in. Tropical forests are disappearing at rates variously estimated at ten to twenty-five, fifty, and up to a hundred acres a minute. The figures cannot be exact and people regularly disagree on the estimates, but the point is that the numbers are always large when added up over a year. Moreover, tropical forests, and the vast numbers of species they shelter, are disappearing at an accelerating rate.

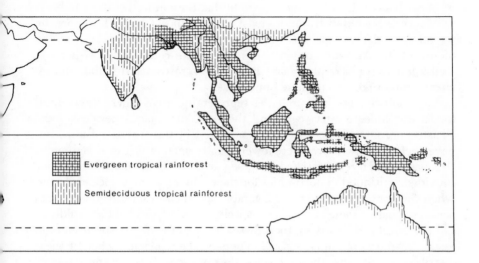

Evergreen tropical rainforest

Semideciduous tropical rainforest

If one is concerned about protecting the large portion of plant and animal life that occurs in these forests, it is important to make some decisions as to where national parks and protected areas should be. Here we run up against a real problem—namely, lack of knowledge. Robert Jenkins will describe later in this symposium how The Nature Conservancy approaches the problem of protecting biological diversity in the United States through its Heritage Programs. Luckily, they have the advantage of a fairly good data base. When it comes to the tropical forests, and perhaps the Amazon most of all, we still lack a good data base, and the problem is how to conserve wisely with this handicap. Only two well-known groups of animals exist in the Amazon Basin, one being butterflies and the other birds. There is a large gap in knowledge about insect life, certainly an integral part of these ecosystems and equally important for conservation. The vast majority of species have never even been examined by a scientist, nor have their distributions been worked out.

At the moment, we are approaching this difficult problem with a theory that may or may not prove valid but, in any case, is useful for us. If one looks at the distributions of the few well-known groups of plants and animals, such as birds, it becomes apparent that pronounced clusters of birds with very restricted distributions exist in the tropical forests. These are the so-called "endemic" species. There is one cluster, for example, near the mouth of the Amazon and another in the south-central area. Other less well-known groups of plants and animals with restricted distributions are clustered more or less in these same areas.

These clusters are interpreted as representing areas where the tropical forest was able to survive during the cold, dry glacial periods of the Pleistocene. Of course, no glaciers occurred in the Amazon Basin, but nevertheless temperatures were lowered and rainfall was less. It is thought that patches of forest persisted in these particular locations, and that they provided continued opportunities for the evolution of new species. Later, when the climate became more favorable and the forests spread out again across the basin, some of those new species did not spread out as rapidly as did the forests. If this is so, then these clusters of endemic species are, in essence, "ghosts of climates past." There is some question whether these distribution patterns, these clusters, do represent "Pleistocene refugia." From the conservationist's viewpoint, this is almost irrelevant. We are concerned with protecting species with restricted distributions because they are the animals and plants most easily threatened with extinction. I hasten to point out that one does not necessarily need to protect the entire area of one of these clusters to protect all the plant and animal species within it.

Current conservation plans for the Amazon Basin are based squarely on these Pleistocene refugia, as defined for birds, butterflies, some reptiles, and four or five families of trees. This is not a very strong data base for making decisions that we hope could eventually protect 10 percent of all the plant and animal species on this planet. If we take one of the higher estimates of total species on the earth, perhaps 10 million species, this means protecting about a million species or so in the Amazon Basin. We must press forward to find ways to increase our knowledge about the plants and animals in the Amazon Basin. And from time to time, we must take second looks at whether our past decisions about sites for national parks and reserves have indeed been as successful as we had hoped.

In dealing with the question of where national parks should be located, I have found that we need to focus greater attention on the question of what the desirable minimum size of a national park should be. It is important to emphasize that habitat is not only being destroyed but is also being fragmented. Figure 2 shows, in four illustrations, the history of the shrinking of coastal forests in the state of Sao Paulo in southern Brazil. The coast of Brazil from the easternmost bulge of South America down to Uruguay is covered by a forest that is distinct from that of the Amazon Basin. We hear less about this forest because the Amazon is so huge and seems so mysterious and romantic that it attracts more attention. But the coastal forests of Brazil are in dire straits—less than 2 percent of them remain. The forest cover in the state of Sao Paulo changed only 2 percent between 1500, the time of the discovery of Brazil, and 1845. In the illustration, note the rapid decline of the forests since 1907. The fourth illustration is a projection for the year 2000, but unfortunately the destruction has moved so rapidly that we are almost there now. Not only is it discouraging, to say the least, to see that much habitat disappear, but it is obvious that frag-mentation also has occurred.

We have become aware, particularly in the last decade, that the biologi-cal dynamics within an isolated fragment of habitat are very different from what they were when the area was still part of an intact large area of forest. Put simply: if one takes a cookie cutter to a large area of forest and trims away around the cookie cutter, leaving only pieces, these forest patches are unable to continue to support the entire array of plant and animal species located there. The alteration begins to occur the moment the cookie cutter or the bulldozer is taken away. As soon as isolation takes place, a whole series of new dynamics is triggered, and species become lost in a kind of ecosystem-decay process.

In the coastal forests of Brazil (Figure 2), one of the best known of the species is the lion tamarin, a spectacular animal numbering perhaps 200 individuals in the wild (Figure 3). The lion tamarin is only one of 17 pri-mates, along with 140 species of birds, that occur only in these coastal for-ests. If one considers plants and insect life, the number of species found only in these forests escalates. The lion tamarin has been bred quite suc-cessfully in captivity here in the National Zoological Park, but the distinct ecosystem of which it is a part could only be preserved on location. We have, in fact, in the coastal forests of Brazil, the frightening potential of seeing one of the first big waves of major extinctions about which various conservationists have been writing.

The phenomenon of forest or other habitat fragmentation raises very se-rious questions about the design and management of national parks. It is fair to ask whether many of the national parks that already exist are ecologically capable of supporting all the species still found within their borders, and whether they can fulfill over a period of time the purposes for which they were originally set up. One way of approaching this question is to study it in terms of actual islands. This comparison has been written

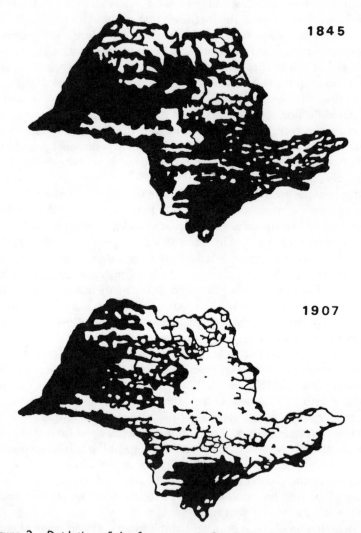

1845

1907

Figure 2   Depletion of the forest area in Sao Paulo, Brazil. Between 1500 and 1845, the area of forest covering the state changed only from 82 percent (20,450 km²) to 80 percent. During this century, the decline has become increasingly rapid, dropping from 58 percent in 1907 to 18 percent in 1952 and to only 8 percent by 1973. At the current rate of forest conversion, only 3 percent or 7,500 km² of Sao Paulo is expected to be covered by forest in the year 2000. Illustration by Kathleen Spagnola, adapted from Oedekoven 1980.

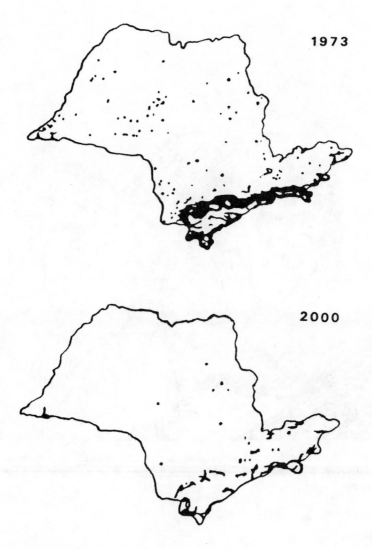

1973

2000

Figure 3   *A golden lion tamarin* (Leontopithetcus rosalia) *adult male carries twin offspring. Illustration by Sigrid J. Bruch, from a photograph by Lawrence Newman.*

about quite extensively in the last few years, particularly with reference to Barro Colorado Island in Panama, which Gene Morton will discuss later in this symposium. If we can study particular bird or mammal species on enough islands of varying size, we can sometimes find that for a particular species there seems to be a threshold island size below which it does not occur and above which it does. This threshold concept indicates that anything over the threshold size would satisfy the conservation requirements for that species. Not all species demonstrate a threshold; some seem to thrive on islands of any size. If one is concerned about protecting entire communities, the question becomes more complex.

The relationship between the size of an area and the number of species it contains has been known to science for some 150 years. Generally speaking, wherever one looks in the world one sees a curve that rises forever: the greater the area, the more species within it. This really does not help us much; it tells us that a large reserve will probably hold more species than a small reserve, but it does not tell us anything about how many species might survive within a particular area.

Plant sociologists in the early part of this century developed information on a "minimum" area, by which they meant an area sufficient to include most of the plant species characteristic to a given community. This work lacked actual ecological dynamics in its definition, and its developers were not thinking about whether that minimum area, if isolated, would hold all the species in the plant community. Somewhere beyond this study is an elusive goal, which I call the "minimum critical size" of an ecosystem. This would be the minimum area within which we would not lose any characteristic species. Let me illustrate: if it is characteristic of central Amazonian forests to have 300 species of trees wherever you sample 10 hectares, we are seeking a national park of sufficient size so that 50, 100, 500, or even 1,000 years from now one could go in and sample any 10 hectares and still come up with essentially the same number of tree species. That number of tree species is characteristic of a biological association, which is one of the things we are trying to protect. We are not just seeking to protect the plant and animal species—we are trying to protect them in their associations, interactions, and processes as well.

Now how does one get at such an elusive question? One approach, as I mentioned, is to study islands. Another approach is available to us because of a fortuitous set of circumstances that exists in Brazil—a law requiring any developer to leave something on the order of 50 percent of his land in forests. This inspired a Brazilian colleague and myself to inquire of the relevant authorities whether they could arrange the layout of those 50 percent forest remnants in a particular area to provide for what will be, in essence, a giant experiment. In our "minimum size" project, we will have a series of forest patches of different sizes left for us in the course of development, which we will have picked out and studied while the forest was still continuous and intact. Before development begins, we can inventory the community in each area and then follow it over the next ten or twenty years as it goes through the ecosystem-decay process, collecting data on the whole exercise. With duplicates and replicates of forest fragments of given sizes, we can gain some notion of which events can be foreseen. Are species lost in a predictable order? Will patches of similar size end up with similar species compositions? We can watch each fragment undergoing its own internal dynamics in the ecosystem-decay process, being supplemented occasionally by colonization or recolonization, until finally we end up with a smaller, simpler, and perhaps more stable species composition. This ecosystem-decay process is really a dominant theme in the way the human presence is affecting the biology of the planet. It is a process that we have only come to appreciate sufficiently in the last ten years, and one that will help us answer important questions as to the size of national parks. It should also aid us in managing smaller parks in such a way that they can hold more species than they otherwise might.

Two particularly good examples of the sorts of relationships that affect minimum size exist. One involves army ants, those almost macabre ants that occur in the New World tropical forests in colonies of a few hundred thousand, or perhaps half-a-million. These ants go through a three-week cycle, during part of which they are in a quiescent, bivouac stage and during the other part of which they are in a swarming stage. When swarming, they move across the floor of the tropical forest in search of insects and other kinds of prey that normally protect themselves by being cryptic in their appearance and remaining very still. When an army-ant colony is advancing across the floor of the forest not only is it quite audible, because there are several hundred thousand ants on the move stirring up leaf litter, but other insects also punctuate the silence by trying to escape. A number of species of birds, such as the fire-eye in the lower Amazon and the white-plumed ant bird in the central Amazon, make their living on a daily basis by following army-ant swarms. In essence, such birds let the ants act as beaters, then swoop down in front of the ants and take some of the prey before the ants get to it. Undoubtedly, a minimum area of forest is necessary to support a minimum number of army-ant colonies so that on any given day a minimum number of the colonies are in swarming state to enable these antbirds to have enough food to feed not only themselves but also their young.

Another example would be pollination systems such as that involving the Brazil nut, a species that has never been grown successfully on plantations. Every Brazil nut ever eaten was taken out of the Amazon Forest. What we normally see as a Brazil nut, even when still in its shell, is only part of a large, baseball-like fruit that contains these nuts. It has a single pollinator. Only one species of bee is capable of getting into its complicated and toughly constructed flower to do this job. And that bee, of course, needs other species of trees to support it during those months of the year when the Brazil nut is not in flower. This requirement implies that a minimum area of forest is needed.

This is the kind of story that is going to be repeated over and over again in tropical forest conservation and, to a lesser but very real degree, in any habitat we try to protect anywhere in the world. Some species are going to be less dependent on a network of other species in the immediate vicinity, or at least they will seem to be. Canopy-dwelling species of the tropical forests, such as macaws, which are good at moving about, may well be able to persist in a checkered landscape where they can easily fly from one patch of forest to the next in search of food. But others, such as birds of the forest interior, will largely be confined to the one patch in which they find themselves.

One interesting result from this project emerged when clearing of the forest began around one of the first of our patches. When the understory was cleared, we had, all of a sudden, a doubling in the capture rate of birds in our nets in the intact piece of forest. We were seeing a major influx of birds from the surrounding areas that were fleeing for refuge into the remnant piece of forest. So it seems that there is not only the problem of the ecosystem-decay process going on after isolation but also an overpopulation problem to begin with. This problem is likely to be more severe for a small reserve than a large one, but it is a dramatic indication of how little we know of the dynamics of isolated fragments if a phenomenon as obvious as this is one of the first things to come to our attention.

Large birds and mammals at the ends of long food chains are especially sensitive. An example found in the Amazon is the Guyana crested eagle. Such predators unquestionably involve special problems for conservationists, yet they are important members of these communities. They have particular ecological roles to play, and if our goal is to maintain the community in a form similar to its natural condition, we want to keep them there. We do not know for even one of these predators what the minimum population size would be to avoid inbreeding problems described earlier in this symposium.

My thesis is that in many instances, and perhaps the majority, species such as the Guyana crested eagle will only be maintainable by some direct, manipulative conservation activity. An example in the United States is the black-footed ferret, which most happily has come to light within the last few years (Figure 4). Its known population has gone from near zero to perhaps 60. This is very encouraging, but, nonetheless, black-footed ferrets may require some special manipulative aids. They live in prairie-dog towns, generally one pair per town, and make their living by preying on prairie dogs. As soon as they produce a litter, the litter must disperse and find other prairie-dog towns. The American West is no longer wall-to-wall prairie-dog towns, which presents special problems in conserving this animal. Probably, direct intervention will be needed to aid black-footed ferrets in dispersing to distant prairie-dog towns.

The dusky seaside sparrow is an interesting example of just how bad conservation problems can become. There are four remaining dusky seaside sparrows in the Cape Canaveral area of Florida, they are all males, and they are all in captivity. A couple of years back, before being brought into captivity, they sang their hearts out in the spring yet no females arrived. There actually is something one can do when the situation gets this bad, and the U.S. Fish and Wildlife Service has agreed to allow it to be done. The remaining male dusky seaside sparrows are being crossed with a closely related form of the dark seaside sparrow, and the progeny will be backbred to the male duskys. If they are successful in doing this a sufficient number of times, they will end up with birds that genetically are mostly "dusky seaside sparrow." They may not capture the entire gene pool—that is hard to do—but they will have saved some of it. My only comment on this is that we will do much better and save many more species if we can work on conservation problems while they are still at the community level, instead of at the level of a few remaining individuals of a single-sex population.

A different set of problems arises when it comes to migratory animals. A single reserve will not be adequate in protecting migratory populations. Probably the most spectacular of all migrations, when all the details are considered, is that of America's best-known butterfly, the Monarch. Only very recently were its wintering grounds, or parts of them, discovered in Mexico. Then the whole story began to be unraveled by a number of scientists, today most actively by Lincoln Brower of the University of Flor-

Figure 4 *The black-footed ferret (Mustela nigripes), once thought extinct, has been rediscovered in Wyoming, where a small population was found and studied in 1981. Illustration by Sally Bensusen.*

ida. It is an extraordinary migration involving three or more generations. Beginning in late October or early November of each year, one generation flies south to the central Mexican mountains where the butterflies spend the winter. This is an extraordinary journey, in itself, for a little creature. If we were designing something that could fly several thousand miles to a precise spot in central Mexico, it is unlikely that the design would be a butterfly.

The wintering grounds are very small areas; ten acres may contain something like twelve million butterflies. These butterfly collectives are most extraordinary to witness. To see one is like being in a snowstorm where the snow is all butterflies. The butterflies spend the winter at this place, requiring a very precise set of conditions, including water. If it gets a couple of degrees colder than the normal temperature within the closed pine and fir forests, they freeze and are gone. Monarch butterflies are a member of a tropical family and cannot withstand freezing temperatures at any stage during their life cycle. On occasion, a wintering concentration has been noted to move up and down a few hundred feet in altitude. No one knows how permanent these wintering spots are.

But the story is even more complicated. Even if we succeed, as I believe we will, in protecting the particular areas where we know the Monarch butterflies winter, we will still have to worry about how they get there and how they make it back. The trip back takes two generations of butterflies, and this is one of the truly fascinating things about this species. No other multigenerational migration is known. The necessary information clearly is passed on from one generation to the next.

Why is the Monarch butterfly able to migrate in the first place? It probably has something to do with the fact that it does not taste very good, at least to birds. An interesting bit of biology has been worked out on this: the butterfly larvae feed on milkweed plants, taking in toxins from the latex of the milkweed, which they store within their bodies. This makes them distasteful and sometimes poisonous to birds. Once a bird has tasted a Monarch butterfly, it may avoid orange butterflies forever after. One thing we now have to worry about is maintaining the distastefulness of the Monarch butterfly. Modern agricultural practices are shifting things in favor of some milkweed species that are not as toxic as the one on which the Monarch butterfly has habitually fed. One of these days, it could well turn out that birds will begin to discover that Monarch butterflies are indeed good to eat, and then this incredible species will be highly imperiled.

These illustrations give some examples of what we have to worry about scientifically to approach conservation on a sound basis. Looking at the

Amazon again, let us suppose we were able to set aside a whole series of reserves throughout the basin; perhaps we can even look at the fresh-water systems and find out where the endemic fish species are (probably in the headwaters of the Amazon) and bring them under protection. Will we have solved the conservation problem? The answer is no.

Other problems need to be solved, and a particular one is interesting because it moves us into the realm of "political" perceptions of conservation issues. There has been a fair amount of speculation and writing about how tropical deforestation may be contributing to the problem of increasing concentrations of carbon dioxide in the atmosphere. The concern is with what this may do to world climate and agricultural productivity in distant regions such as the grain-growing belts, including the major one in the United States. The potential impact of this problem might not be perceived in Brazil as a high-priority issue with direct consequences in the short-run. However, another phenomenon might be so perceived. For the first time in history, good scientific evidence shows that forests not only can attract rainfall but can also produce it. We know that nearly half of all the rainfall in the Amazon Basin is generated by the forest itself. Studies done by isotope analysis of rainfall across the Amazon Basin led to a workshop on this topic in the south of Brazil. The workshop was cosponsored by an unlikely marriage of the World Wildlife Fund and the International Atomic Energy Agency (Salati, Lovejoy, and Vose 1983). This scientific evidence indicates that if too much of the Amazon Basin is converted to nonforests, it is distinctly possible that an irreversible drying trend could be triggered there. That would mean that every one of our conservation projects in the area would be in trouble. It would also mean that every other biologically based activity of mankind in the Amazon Basin would be affected by climatic change. This phenomenon probably would be perceived by Brazilians as a major issue.

To conclude, I want to mention two examples of other ways in which the tropical forests might be important. Most of us are aware of how particular species or natural processes can benefit human beings. Many people are unaware, however, that the tropical forest is one of the champion nutrient recycling systems in the world. We assume that because they are so luxuriant they spring from rich soil. In fact, these forests, because of their nutrient recycling capacity, are able to grow on top of some of the poorest soils in the world. This is one of the great paradoxes in nature. It occurs because of the rapid decomposition of organic matter through the action of soil animals and plants—fungi, bacteria, termites, earthworms—in complex chemical and mechanical ways. Some trees even thrust their roots directly into fallen trees to extract their nutrients. Nutrients are what agriculture is all about, and anything we can learn from the tropical forests about how to improve nutrient recycling is obviously of considerable consequence for agriculture and a wide range of other human biological activities, including forestry.

The second example has to do with the leaf-cutting ant that inhabits these forests. This species was known until recently as either a biological curiosity (for scientists) or as a mere pest (by those trying to keep a garden going). These ants, which have very large nests, can defoliate a particular tree overnight. They do not eat the leaves but take all the pieces of leaves down into their nests and use them as mulch for farming a fungus they do eat. There had been considerable speculation over the years as to why leaf-cutting ants chose only particular tree species to defoliate—and not all trees. Perhaps they avoided trees that had distasteful compounds in their leaves. In the last year, this avoidance has turned out to have quite a different explanation, one that is very obvious if one thinks about it. Trees that leaf-cutting ants avoid turn out to be those that have natural fungicides in their leaves. Such chemicals are a logical thing for most trees to have in a tropical forest. With all that moisture around, the fungus problem is a serious one. And all too logically, it makes little sense to import fungicides into a fungus farm! This discovery gives science an immediate key to identifying species of trees likely to contain natural fungicides. This finding could be useful for mankind in a variety of ways and may someday be useful in agriculture. The scientists at the University of Iowa who discovered this were able to make the point that such fungicides might benefit the state of Iowa. I would like to end merely by pointing out that the first time we discovered a natural fungicide, it turned out to be penicillin.

References Cited and Additional Readings

Grzimek, B.
  1974.   *Grzimek's Animal Life Encyclopedia* (13 vols.). New York: Van Nostrand Reinhold Co.
  1976.   *Grzimek's Encyclopedia of Ecology*. New York: Van Nostrand Reinhold Co.

IUCN (International Union for Conservation of Nature and Natural Resources).
  1980.   *World Conservation Strategy*. IUCN, Morges, Switzerland.

Oedekoven, K. I.
   1980.   The vanishing forest. *Environmental Policy and Law* 6 (4):
            184–85.

Salati, E., T. E. Lovejoy, and P. B. Vose.
   1983.   Precipitation and water recycling in tropical rainforests with spe-
            cial reference to the Amazon Basin. *Environmentalist* 3:67–72.

8

Sustainable Exploitation Of Wildlife
As A Strategy Toward Enhanced Conservation

N O R M A N   M Y E R S

I want to describe my experiences in East Africa during the past 25 years and some of the changes that I have seen there. My remarks are primarily geared to Kenya, but they can be broadly applied to several other countries of savannah Africa.

While some of my ideas on controlled exploitation of wildlife are, I like to think, innovative, I want to mention, front and center, that I am not suggesting that they be applied as a blanket approach across Africa. My proposals are intended to supplement approaches that have already been applied—not to supplant them. Others are also examining fresh conservation strategies. Just this morning, I picked up a copy of the *New York Times* (September 12, 1982), and the magazine section had a lead story on "exploitation" of African wildlife as a valid conservation strategy. Now I did not write the piece, and I had nothing to do with its timing. But I recommend it to you because it goes into this whole topic in considerable detail. You will find in it opinions of conservationists, white and black, people who have lived in Africa a good deal longer than I have, and people who have been there only as visitors for a few months. It includes opinions of scientists, wildlife managers, government officials, and leaders of conservation groups, and their common conclusion is that the wildlife scene in Kenya is in trouble, a lot of trouble. They differ on how we should respond to this worsening situation. But there does seem to be a consensus that what has worked hitherto is no longer working nearly so well. They also seem to agree that continuing a strategy of "the same as before, only more so" also may not work so well. Thus, we need to search out and examine some new approaches to bolster those we have had in the past.

Among the persons cited in the *New York Times* article are representatives of two organizations that have done a great deal for the cause of African wildlife during the past 20 or 25 years. One is the World Wildlife Fund, and we have just heard from Dr. Tom Lovejoy, who is vice president for Science, World Wildlife Fund-USA. The World Wildlife Fund has an exemplary record in Africa; it was one of the conservation movement's pioneers and has done a great job there. The other organization is the African Wildlife Leadership Foundation, whose efforts are focused primarily on savannah Africa. These two organizations should be commended for the work they have been doing in Kenya.

Two months ago, I went on a safari in Kenya. It was a very sad safari because at its conclusion I was leaving Kenya for the last time after being there for many years. I have wondered during the last few weeks why it is that I felt such a strong attachment to Kenya. The reason is probably clear from an incident that occurred three or four months ago when I was engaged in a round of final safaris with my wife and two children. We went to Amboseli, a park at the foot of Kilamanjaro, that has a tremendous concentration of wildlife. The snows of Kilamanjaro feed the swamps and waterholes of Amboseli, which are oases for the wildlife that graze and browse in its rather dry countryside. Despite the dryness, the vegetation sustains large numbers of animals in exceptional variety. We got up about six in the morning and set off to go trundling about. We came around a corner in our safari truck, and there in the middle of the plain, just 30 yards away, was a giraffe. Now a giraffe is no big potatoes in the pecking order of African wildlife, and you may feel that it does not have the charisma of a lion or an elephant. It was just a common old giraffe. It stood there and stared at us from those huge, soft, liquid eyes, and from under those outrageous eyelashes. It just looked at us and we looked back. After a while, the giraffe had looked enough, and it turned quietly away to go on browsing. I felt at the time that this is what African wildlife is all about. Here is this big creature that intends us no harm, just looks with curiosity at us in our strange box riding around in the middle of a game park; here is this giraffe that can go about its business free and untrammeled, as it has been doing for thousands of years. How fine it would be if it could continue to do that. The following week, I was trying to complete another book, *A Wealth of Wild Species* [published in 1983]. I had been debating how to conclude it. I sat down then and wrote the last few pages; how when I had left Kenya and had gone to live in England, it would be OK living there if, when I went out jogging or just walking with the children, I could recall that one day in Amboseli and could hope that around the next corner I might come face to face with a deer or some other creature. I wrote that if I could feel that this could happen, then all would be well. This is what wildlife means to me. That is what I have been told by these large animals of East Africa. It is a very big gift from them, and it matters far more to me than all the photographs I have ever taken. When my children are grown up, in the year 2000, I would like to think that there will still be giraffes in East Africa for us all to enjoy.

But I doubt it. The world is closing in on the wildlife of East Africa very quickly. The areas of wildlife we have now in the early 1980s, compared to what we had, say, at the end of the Second World War, is perhaps one-tenth. And what we had then was about one-tenth of what there was at the beginning of the 1800s. What we have now is a mere fragment of what there used to be. It is true, as we heard from Professor Stanley, that the spectacle of wildlife in East Africa in modern times is itself only a small remnant of what it was at the height of the Pleistocene, maybe 50,000 or 100,000 years ago. But be that as it may, what we still see in these African plains represents the most diversified and spectacular array of large mammal life still available on the face of this planet. We have seen it on television, and we have seen it in the *National Geographic* and other magazines. However, it is something like Niagara Falls and the Grand Canyon; no matter how many photographs you see, you can not really grasp or sense the scale and impact of this spectacle until you are right there and can see it for yourself. Because the prospect exists that this spectacle may be going under, maybe we should start to mobilize all our resources, meaning especially our imaginations, to try to devise some strategy to safeguard what little bit we can.

When I first went to East Africa in the late 1950s, I remember that as we approached Nairobi Airport the plane did not come straight in to land. We circled two or three times around the airstrip to shoo out of the way a bunch of buffalos that were lying down in the middle of the runway. We got the buffalos out of the way and the plane landed. In those days, there was a longish walk to the airport terminal, and two- or three-hundred yards away, right by the edge of the terminal, were—I blinked my eyes, but there they were—two big black-maned lions. And on the way from the airport into the middle of Nairobi, we passed quite large herds of zebras and wildebeest. When we reached downtown Nairobi, we stopped at a post office by a little freeway running through town. There on the grass strip that ran down the middle of the freeway was a herd of gazelles grazing. That is the way Kenya was in the late 1950s. In those days, it was a sea of wild lands with little islands of human settlements.

Now it is the other way around. Kenya is becoming a sea of human settlements with little islands, pockets of wildlife. The question is whether these islands can survive the next 20 years. I am not talking about whether they can survive the next 200 years, or the next 20,000 years, because 20 years is the time horizon that we have to talk about.

Human presence aside, it is incorrect to suppose that wildlife makes its home right across Africa from one ocean to the other. The wildlife is most concentrated in woodland and grassland savannahs. The other main areas, the tropical forests and the arid lands, are not home to the large herbivores with which you are most familiar—the wildebeest, zebras, giraffes, and similar creatures. Indeed, of all of Africa south of the Sahara, less than 10 percent can be classified as good-quality wildlife country. It is in the major parks of Kenya, Tanzania, Uganda, Zambia, Zimbabwe, and South Africa that you will see the most exceptional variety of herbivores and, of course, predators. As for birds, it is not difficult to check at least 20 or 30 or sometimes as many as 50 species of birds in a single day in one of these major parks.

What kinds of pressures are threatening these spectacles, and how fast are the threats gathering? The main problem lies with human populations—not only the growth in human numbers but also the growth in human aspirations. And these twin phenomena working side-by-side and reinforcing each other have already reached a pitch, because of which several major parks in Kenya are being subjected to what we might call the "salami treatment." The Amboseli Park, which I feel, having visited over 200 parks in Africa, is the finest park in Africa, is about to lose 5 percent of its territory to the local Masai. Now 5 percent may be restored to a different sector, but all the same this loss is a sign of the times. The Masai Mara Game Reserve in western Kenya, being the northern extension of the Serengeti ecosystem, has already lost 5 percent of its territory this year and is scheduled to lose another 10 percent of its territory to stock raisers by the end of the year. The enormous Tsavo Park—8,000 square miles, the size of Vermont or New Hampshire, and one of the biggest parks in the whole world—is being subjected to an agonizing array of appraisals by a number of planners in Kenya. Within the next few years, it will probably lose one-quarter, possibly one-third, and even conceivably one-half of its area to land-hungry people in the environs.

Now this is not to say that the Kenyan government is reneging on its basic commitment to wildlife. The problem that the government faces is that there are just too many people who are clamouring for a place to sink a digging hoe and raise their subsistence crops of maize or cassava or rice. Let me give a brief review of the Kenyan government's track record. I mentioned earlier that 6 percent of its national territory is currently under protected status in the form of parks or reserves. That is twice as much as the country had when it achieved independence in 1963. About two years ago, the World Bank, together with the government of Kenya, developed a wildlife conservation project that will become worth $34 million during the course of the 1980s. Half of the $34 million is being loaned (not donated, but loaned) by the World Bank, and the other $17 million is being raised by Kenya. Now anyone can do the following arithmetic: among the 17 million people in Kenya, about 1 person in 10 is a taxpayer; the average cash income of people in Kenya is about $400 a year. So Kenyans are going to have to dig pretty deep into their pockets to raise the $17 million in counterpart funds to match the loan from the World Bank. That is a measure of the commitment of the Kenyan government and citizenry to the cause of wildlife there.

But at the same time, there are too many Kenyans for the country to support. Kenyans are pressing right up against the borders of these parks, and they are demanding that part of the parks be given over to them so they can grow their crops and raise their cattle. Such are the pressures being generated by the present 17 million people. Before long, Kenya is going to have a lot more people. The country has an annual population growth rate of 4 percent, the highest ever recorded for any human community on the face of the earth, and the rate is still rising. Kenya is not the only country in Africa with a high population growth rate. Several others have reached 3.5 percent and are still increasing; they will soon be going through the "4 percent barrier," as you might call it. The average rate of growth for sub-Saharan Africa is about 3.2 percent. This contrasts with an average growth rate for the entire developing world of 2.5 percent. Complex and powerful forces underlie the high population growth rate of sub-Saharan Africa, and it is going to be extremely difficult to turn the situation around.

Two factors determine a country's population outlook. One is its existing population growth rate. The other, which counts far more for its future, is called its demographic "profile"—the proportions of the population in three categories: the elderly, young adults, and youngsters. In the United States, for example, the people in that third group, age 15 or less, constitute about 21 percent of the total. In most developing countries, that group constitutes 35 to 50 percent. In Kenya this group constitutes 55 to

58 percent of the current population of 17 million. This means that a huge number of the potential parents of the future have already been born. How does this affect the future population outlook? If Kenyan families could be persuaded right now to have only two children per family, the population would keep on growing for at least another two generations and would surpass forty million people somewhere well into the next century. But of course, this 55 to 58 percent of Kenya's population is not going to decide to limit itself to two children per family, especially when the average figure is already eight- and one-half children per family and still rising. With the current pattern of family size and 4 percent growth rate, Kenya's population will roughly double by the year 2000, or in less than 20 years. And if the population keeps on growing at that rate, then within 100 years it will have increased 19 times because of the compound effect. The World Bank recently produced some population projections of this sort for growth rates in Africa. Even allowing for more effective family-planning programs than are now in operation, it is thought that the population of Africa, currently less than 500 million, will more than quadruple, reaching perhaps 2.2 billion before it finally levels out and stabilizes.

Well, those are some of the projected figures. But Kenya is already bursting at the seams in supporting its 17-million people. In my view, it is not going to be possible to support even 30-million people, no matter what technological miracles may occur or how much foreign aid is available. If that number is reached there will, I fear, be mass starvation in Kenya. This is a dreadful thought, an awful prospect. But that is the way it could be in Kenya and other African countries as well. The cause of wildlife would of course not be assisted by such a tragedy either because when people are starving they will do anything to find a patch of ground on which to grow food. If an area of a thousand square miles, such as the Masai Mara Game Reserve, has a tolerable rainfall, and the people of Kenya are told that this thousand square miles is inviolable—to produce zebras and wildebeest for the sake of tourism or to safeguard a world natural heritage or to benefit future generations—those starving people are going to say, "How is that again, tourism, future generations?" They won't get so far as to ask such a question; they will want to get in there. I believe that if the Kenyan government were to post an armed guard at one-yard intervals right around that Mara Game Reserve, it would still not keep out starving throngs of Kenyans. That is why 5 percent of this area has already been taken off and why another 10 percent will likely be taken off by the end of this year or next.

I suggest that the one way we can safeguard the future of these parks now is by enabling them to produce something valuable to those living at their borders, and that means food, above all. If the Masai Mara Game Reserve could be demonstrated now as one of the finest meat-producing areas in the whole of Africa, in the whole of the world even, then I believe Kenyans might be persuaded to keep out of it—if that food were available to them. Unless this happens, I would not bet a single dime on the survival of the Mara Game Reserve, not even until the end of this century, let alone into the next.

What can we do in practical terms to assist these parks and reserves to meet the needs of local Africans, especially in terms of food? There are various ways. When I was United Nations' park and wildlife officer for the whole of Africa in the mid-1970s, I traveled around Africa, visiting 40 countries. I looked at more than 200 parks and reserves, and many of them were under pressure. But quite a few of them, I noticed, did not seem to be under very much pressure, even though lots of people were in the environs. So after I had spent a day roaming around a park with its warden, we would go in the evening to villages outside the park and have a beer or two in the local bar. We would say to the local people, "Hey folks, what do you think about this park?" And instead of saying, in effect, that it was an alien enclave in their own back yards, these local people would say, "Well, it seems OK, we get our share of the action out of it." Getting further into the subject, it would turn out that the park warden was allowing local people to practice various forms of exploitation inside the park or reserve. In some cases, it would be fishing in local lakes or rivers or sometimes in the catchments of artificial dams where waterholes had been established for wildlife. In fact, the wardens would introduce fish into these lakes or reservoirs, and local people would come along and take their annual harvest. They really liked the animal protein they were getting in the form of those fish. Bear in mind, that an African receives, on average, less animal protein, less meat per week, than does a domestic cat in this country. So fishing is one good way to exploit the parks. Yet it is exploitation that is, strictly speaking, against the rules. A park or reserve is not supposed to permit any kind of exploitation whatsoever for human purposes. But fishing does not do too much harm. It does not upset the tourists; they do not generally go looking for fishes, and if they did, they would not be able to photograph them.

Other forms of exploitation are also practiced now. One is dry-season grazing for the relief of domestic livestock. There are some parks where, for example, from August to November the wildlife moves off to one area and other large areas of range land are left more or less unoccupied. This affords an opportunity for local people to take their cattle inside for relief grazing if the park warden permits it. Again, this is strictly against the rules: a park may not allow any kind of exploitation of that kind for any reason whatsoever. This was done for a time in Serengeti but was discontinued, no doubt in fear of protest from park experts in Europe or North America. The local people are becoming rather disenchanted with the Serengeti.

Another form of exploitation practiced is subsistence hunting, otherwise known as poaching. But if hunting by local people can be permitted and properly regulated, which we know from experience is possible, then it can help meet the needs of local people and help to defuse the antagonism that may have arisen because a large chunk of territory has been locked away. It works this way: local people are allowed into the park, perhaps on the second Tuesday of each month—that is all. They are allowed to hunt with bows and arrows or spears—that is all. They may not bring in firearms and therefore cannot kill very many animals. They are allowed in on just that one day, and they will be able to take only enough meat to satisfy their needs. The number of animals they take on one day a month is not really going to affect the long-term health and survival capacity of the wild herds, so it works for both sides.

Other forms of exploitation, such as sport hunting, are very much against the rules. These are being practiced in the Selous Game Reserve in southern Tanzania and in some other reserves that have much better prospects of surviving into the next century than does the Masai Mara Game Reserve.

The final form of exploitation practiced is one that really raises the hackles of some conservationists. This is commercial exploitation for meat and, in the case of some creatures, for trophies. It is true that a few zebras, wildebeest, hippos, elephants, gazelles, buffalos, and giraffes can be killed through controlled cropping without threatening any of these species' survival. We know from experience that if we take 10 percent of these creatures during the year, the 90 percent that survive will procreate and by the next year will have made up their numbers, at which point the cropper can take a further 10 percent harvest during the next year. Biologically, we know that it can be done, that it is feasible for the wild herds. Obviously, we are not talking about endangered species. So technologically, it is possible to get thousands of wild animals off the hoof and into cans, and to have the cans distributed around the countryside in local African markets. Another way is to kill the animals and call in the local butchers who arrive with their flatbed trucks, take away the big chunks of meat, and sell them the same day. Africans will come from many miles around to take advantage of schemes such as this, which have been implemented not just in Kenya but in Uganda, Zimbabwe, and South Africa. Visitors to the Kruger Park in South Africa may not be aware that while they are tucked up in bed in their safari lodge, people have gone out with big flatbed trucks and killed quite a few dozen buffalos, giraffes, zebras, or elephants, and that they have loaded the carcasses onto the trucks and taken them to the canning factory before daybreak. The tourists go out the next day and look at the herds, take their pictures, and enjoy the wildlife spectacle just the same. If you go to Ngorongoro Crater in northern Tanzania, you sit down for supper in the wildlife lodge there with a choice of wildebeest steak, zebra cutlet, or gazelle goulash, the animals having been taken from the extensive wildlife assemblies in the crater.

Now let us come back for a moment to the Masai Mara Game Reserve, which I mentioned as one of the areas most threatened by human pressures because it has good rainfall and can support ordinary agriculture. It is the northerly extension of the Serengeti ecosystem, of which you have heard so much and seen so often on television. The Serengeti ecosystem is about 10,000 square miles, altogether of which the Mara, where the system extends into Kenya, is about 1,000 square miles. In those 10,000 square miles there are two-million wildebeest, one-and-one-half-million Thompson's gazelles, one-quarter-million zebras and at least one-quarter-million other gazelles, buffalos, impalas, or giraffes. I have seen other throngs, for example, in Alaska, but they do not remotely match it. In the entire United States, some three-and-one-half-million square miles, when you count up all the large mammals—the white-tailed deer, moose, wapiti, bison, pronghorn, caribou, right down the roster—you can list somewhere between 16- and 20-million large animals. In contrast, the Serengeti-Mara ecosystem has 4-million animals in just that 10,000 square miles.

On the western borders of Serengeti and Mara, the human population is building up at a rate not of 4 percent a year but of 8 percent a year, not only because of normal fertility but because of immigration. People are coming from other parts of Tanzania and Kenya to gather in those border zones where there is enough rainfall to grow crops. The question is: how long will they stay outside? How long will it be before these people feel that they really want to get inside the park? Now if we were to route the Serengeti migration through a canning factory, and we took about 10 percent of those herds, we could produce enough meat to go a long way to satisfy the nutritional deficiencies of many millions of Africans. If we just consider the 2-million wildebeest, that 10 percent harvest is 200,000 animals. Each wildebeest produces at least 200 pounds of good, usable meat. That is a lot of one-pound tins of meat—forty-million tins—that can go on the local market. In the case of zebras, you get a lot more meat per animal, and you also get a handsome skin that could retail on the streets of Manhattan for between $600 and $1,000 if the regulations were to permit its sale. This kind of controlled cropping could produce a lot of good solid meat and a lot of good solid profits for the conservation cause.

Let me now wind up this talk by emphasizing that what I am proposing in the way of exploitation of the wildlife spectacle is something that I propose with extreme reluctance. Viewed by itself, it is an awful prospect to have to come to terms with this problem by harvesting wild animals. Whatever the rationale, we view it with repugnance, dismay, and sorrow. Frankly, I can not see any other approach that is going to work, and if one reads the article in the *New York Times* that I mentioned one will find that nine out of ten of those people are advocating a similar approach—a horrendous compromise, if you will. A dreadful response to a dreadful problem. I do not advocate it with any enthusiasm at all. I advocate it only because I do not see what other options we have. We have allowed ourselves in the twentieth century to get backed into a corner with hardly any options. Sticking to our present policies and awaiting the disaster is no option.

Perhaps I should describe to you a scene I once witnessed of cropping at work, back in 1970 when I was completing the first of my books, "The Long African Day." I was sitting at my consultant's desk in Nairobi working out neat calculations on population growth, land-use pressures, park space, elephant numbers, and all those things. I had produced a sophisticated little equation showing that if we crop such-and-such numbers of elephants and produce such-and-such pounds of meat and dollars of revenue from the hides and so on, this could help resolve the critical questions of conservation. It all looked so straightforward there on the sheet of paper. Now one of the colleagues whom I had been consulting about this said, "Why don't you come with us on one of our cropping exercises to see how we do it?" He had pioneered the cropping technique in Africa and had worked out a way to do it with extreme efficiency and dispatch, and with the least possible suffering to the animals. His technique really made an effectual job of a dreadful challenge. So I went with him on a cropping exercise at Tsavo Park, where I joined him and his team in his camp one evening. They said, "Tomorrow morning we will have to get up early before it gets light because with the first few rays of sunlight we shall be up in our helicopter looking for a herd of elephants." The "herd" can be anything from one isolated elephant to several elephants up to a whole herd of 20 with males, females, calves, the whole lot (Figure 1). Occasionally, there may be as many as 30 in the herd. The larger the herd, the more complicated the task. The cropper has to get all those elephants on the ground as fast as he can because if just one or two elephants escape, and elephants can move pretty fast, they will somehow pass the message of fear to neighboring herds. This induces extreme nervousness and anxiety among the elephants in the surrounding areas, who moreover might then vent their feelings on the next safari truck they meet. The rule is, then, that all the elephants in a herd must be brought down. No elephant must be allowed to escape for whatever reason. I am describing all this in rather clinical terms. What else is there to do? That is the way it is.

When we took off in our helicopter, we had three riflemen and three gun bearers to assist them. After about five minutes, we came across a herd of elephants, 27 in all. There were a number of females—the old matriarchs, grannies, and cows—a few males, and quite a lot of little ones less than a year old. The croppers used the helicopter to shoo the elephants together. They then came down low over the herd, the elephants of course began to get excited and apprehensive, and they then crowded together as is the way of elephants. The helicopter was used to bring the elephants out of the thickets into the open. Then the helicopter flew away for a quarter of a mile or so, downwind where the elephants would not hear it. It came down and we all got out and started to approach the herd. The technique when trying to shoot an elephant is to get as close as you can, and then get ten yards closer. We tiptoed through the open, downwind, until we were as close to them as from where I am standing to the back of this auditorium. Then the head of the cropping team checked with his colleagues: were they all ready? Yes, they were all ready. So he gave the signal. I was standing just there, and the noise almost blew my head off. As I tell this now, I can remember it so vividly. I can visualize a tree over there and what the gunman was wearing and the puffs of smoke and how the elephants were distributed. As soon as the first gunman started firing, the other two joined in and went bang, bang, bang, bang, and I could hardly believe that there could be such a bedlam of sound coming from just a few human beings. Then, within two seconds, the bedlam of sound from humans was drowned out by a greater bedlam of sound from the elephants—the ones that were hit. The ones that were not hit were also screaming. They were not just trumpeting, they were screaming. And when elephants make as much noise as they can because they are very frightened, the noise is as if the whole air, the whole earth, is being torn apart. The

Figure 1   *A small herd of African elephants (Loxodonta africana). Illustration by Kathleen Spagnola.*

noise engulfed us. I could not believe that there could be so much noise, and that it could be sustained like that.

But it was not sustained for long. In 45 seconds the noise suddenly came to an end. It was so sudden that it was as if someone had taken a huge ax and chopped the noise off. The noise had come to an end because there was no more firing and no more screaming from elephants. All that was left was a great pile of carcasses. And there was so much silence. Then I did hear something else. It was like a little creek running, a little gurgling. I looked at the big pile of elephants that had been so crowded together that some had fallen on top of each other. There were fountains of blood rushing out and running down the carcasses. That was what was causing the gurgling. And that lasted a couple of minutes or so. Then these fellows went about their business to tackle the carcasses, and I went away and sat under a tree.

The next day I went back to my office in Nairobi. I looked at all those sheets that I had written about how rational and commonsensical it was to crop elephants, and I did not add another word to those sheets for another seven months. And I still ask myself: is that really the best way that we can devise to assist the cause of African wildlife? Do we really have to start perpetrating scenes like that on a large scale, on these wild creatures that have gone their own way for millions of years, just because it suits the exigencies of human populations and because we are trying our best to serve wildlife's interests. Is this what we have to do?

As I mentioned, that was in 1970. Here we are more than a decade later. I have often visualized that scene. And I still can not think of any better way. I wish there were a better way, but I do not know where one looks for it. I have described the situation. I would like to hope that we could have an informed public debate such as I tried to raise a few years ago in the magazine *International Wildlife* (Myers 1976). Of course, when one visualizes actual scenes such as the one I have just described, it is very hard to engage in a dispassionate public debate. But that, I think, is what we urgently need.

References Cited and Recommended Readings

Myers, N.
    1976.   Elephants under the gun. *International Wildlife* Vol. 6, No. 6, 4–16.
    1983.   *A Wealth of Wild Species: Storehouse for Human Welfare.* Boulder, Colo.: Westview Press.

9

The Identification, Acquisition, And Preservation Of Land As A Species Conservation Strategy

ROBERT E. JENKINS, JR.

I will describe here today the conservation strategy that is incorporated into the work of The Nature Conservancy. But I can not proceed without a moment of philosophical reflection. Although most of what I am going to say is objectively detached, I want to join with Drs. Lovejoy and Myers to express my own view that the human species is lurching and stumbling toward a biological catastrophe of the first order. None of us can be certain that the means will be found to avoid it.

Quite clearly, our main problem is an inability to govern ourselves. In discussing the population increase in Kenya, Dr. Myers spoke of a 19-fold increase in human numbers over the next 100 years, given a 3 percent growth rate; but at the current rate of 4 percent, the increase would more likely be 50-fold. Unquestionably, the kinds of solutions suggested for African wildlife, grimly compromising as they appear even in the short-run, will be utterly overtaken by that kind of population pressure.

What The Nature Conservancy does is not itself a permanent solution to such problems, even here in America. We, too, are frustrated by our collective inability to come up with answers to the human governance problem. So we are attempting to duck the problem, to come up with stop-gap measures for the immediate future while long-term solutions can be sought.

The Nature Conservancy is focused entirely on preserving natural ecological diversity by *in situ* conservation—that is, by preserving selected land areas. We work mostly in the United States, although we are increasing our international activities as well. To tell the truth, I am grateful that we have the luxury, so-to-speak, of developing our programs in North

America rather than in places like East Africa. Here we have a temperate climate and a relatively undiverse biota, our ecosystems have a good deal of resilience to artificial disruptions, and we live in a country with only a moderately explosive rate of human population increase.

Considerable biological land conservation has already been accomplished in the United States. The conservancy, along with a number of cooperating institutions, is involved in fine-tuning the expansion of our overall system of preserved lands. This is important because most land conservation in the United States, including the establishment of our national parks and national wildlife refuges, has not been undertaken in such a way that would preserve the full representation of our native habitats and ecosystems. Even today, the need to preserve samples of unrepresented ecosystems is not a main determinant in the establishment of new national parks and refuges.

In some instances, the lands already conserved have been set aside chiefly because they were the most remote, or the least exploitable. In other instances, the lands have been set aside strictly for aesthetic landscapes and spectacular scenic areas. The lands we have preserved contain certain kinds of ecosystems and plant and animal species in abundance. Unfortunately, other kinds of systems of equal biological importance have been neglected because of their scenic drabness or because their plant and animal species are less obvious or appealing. Thus, in spite of all the past land conservation in this country, plenty of organisms are still in trouble.

Because animal species are the subject of this symposium, I will focus on species rather than on whole biotic communities and on animals rather than plants. But, in fact, it is crucial to preserve as much of our total biological, ecological, and genetic diversity as we can.

As I describe the way The Nature Conservancy goes about its work of preserving natural diversity, I will go into considerable detail to make a point. Most of the important things done in conservation—and no doubt other fields of endeavor—involve some careful and detailed work. There are a million tedious details behind the sweeping generalities. Imagine the complexity of our space program. The world we live in is much more complicated than space and could benefit from similarly sophisticated managerial efforts. To editorialize, our conservation profession often seems particularly populated with people who are full of general ideas but who do not know how or are unwilling to get down to detailed operational work.

Over the last 30 years, The Nature Conservancy has acquired and protected more than 3,000 parcels of land, many of which contain significant habitat for endangered animals or plants. We pursue this objective as carefully as we can by a three-step process of identification, protection, and stewardship. My own major responsibility at the conservancy concerns the identification phase.

It turns out to be both difficult and costly to adequately identify priority natural lands for conservation. If we were dealing with a blank slate, with no history of biological conservation or destruction, we could proceed on a much coarser basis. Relatively random land-conservation decisions could produce solid benefits using coarse criteria and a modest investment in the task of identification. This may be the situation in parts of some developing countries even today, but diminishing returns set in when the process of land conservation and destruction is well advanced. By statistical accident, the continuation of random conservation duplicates the most common and widespread kinds of species, habitats, and communities, while failing to capture those that are rare and in some danger. To circumvent this, we need a great deal of information and analysis.

STATE NATURAL HERITAGE INVENTORIES

Although much field research has been done in this country, the results are widely scattered through museum collections, papers in many journals, and agency files that come in an incomprehensible variety of forms. This disorganization prevents our using existing information effectively to ask important questions about conservation needs or data gaps in our current knowledge base.

As a consequence, the conservancy has embarked, in cooperation with state governments, on a relatively large-scale information reorganization effort now known as State Natural Heritage Inventories. Over the last seven or eight years, we have helped to establish more than thirty such programs covering most of the United States. If the current economic situation does not interrupt this process, we should gradually complete the task of developing a nationwide system that provides a comprehensive overview of U.S. conservation needs and opportunities.

The objective of heritage inventories is to accumulate and organize information about what we call the "elements of ecological diversity" and to determine from this which parts of our landscape contribute the most to their perpetuation. These "elements" include all of the recognizable community or ecosystem types as well as the habitats of all rare or endangered species. Most earlier conservation inventories focused on individual sites rather than on the biological and ecological elements themselves. As a result, overmuch importance was attached to whatever areas various people had already alleged to be significant. Such compilations of opinion were heavily biased toward scenery, emotional appeal, and accessibility or remoteness rather than toward ecological qualities per se. Therefore, there was little to guarantee that all ecosystems and habitats would be well represented. By allowing preliminary recommendations about particular land areas to determine data collection priorities, an incomprehensible muddle was made out of the biological information.

After a great deal of trial and error, and repeating many of these same mistakes ourselves, we discovered that what we needed initially was simple and straightforward—to put together a data base on the individual biological and ecological elements rather than on a predetermined list of land areas. Heritage data bases therefore contain information on the existence, characteristics, numbers, condition, status, location, and distribution of the individual species and communities. These data are then analyzed to identify land areas that have the greatest significance for conservation.

Our intent is to list and classify the "elements" of diversity in a way that will capture the entire array of our biological, genetic, and ecological resources. To do this, we use a "coarse filter/fine filter" approach. We look at fairly widely defined natural terrestrial and aquatic communities as coarse filters through which we will reliably capture the majority of species, ecological assemblages, and phenomena (the more abundant ones) of an area. As our main fine filter, we use "special" plant and animal species. Special species are those that are rare, highly specialized, or have other characteristics that make their occurrence unpredictable from coarsely defined community information alone. By using both a typological community classification and a special species list, we hope to capture efficiently the full diversity of our biota and ecosystems.

To maximize efficiency in collecting information, we first concentrate on secondary sources, gradually putting together an organized data base, which is cyclically enlarged and updated. This is what scientists call the literature review stage of research preparation. We examine the existing publications, museum collections, available field notes and files, and maps derived from remote imagery or aerial reconnaissance. Then we interview individual experts for specific unpublished information. A cyclical refinement process eventually takes us into the field. We go afield to confirm the continued existence of species and communities that the secondary information has pinpointed and that comparative analysis has shown to be especially worthy. Finally, we search likely areas of the landscape for potential occurrences of those species and communities that existing information indicates are the rarest or least adequately known.

Information derived from all these sources is compiled rather tediously into a combination of manual files, computerized records, and maps. Maps are especially important in our work. As we integrate this information, we identify the actual localities on the landscape where the special species and communities still persist. We plot these localities on 7.5- and 15-minute quadrangular topographic maps produced by the U.S. Geological Survey. The importance of doing this to establish a data base, especially for endangered species, is so self-evident that it is hard to see how else one could proceed.

However, frequently this is not what has been done. In far too many instances, attempts have been made to characterize the supposed habitat of an endangered species and to look for indirect evidence of the habitat type before calculating the chances that the species might actually occur there. This has not worked very well. Rare and endangered species usually occur in few places, for reasons we often cannot fathom, and they simply do not occupy very much of what looks to us to be suitable habitat. Therefore, elaborate attempts to amass and analyze information on seemingly suitable habitats have usually not panned out. For most endangered organisms, until we know where they actually are, we do not really know anything. When the question is raised regarding the best means to avert the destruction of a species, we may only have information on seemingly suitable habitats. In such cases, we are not in a position to be very helpful. The Heritage inventories are being developed to identify this most basic fact about each rare or endangered species—the specific places where it currently occurs.

Heritage data bases are used for two main purposes. One is as a guide to information needs. We must allocate our limited resources efficiently, so we want our data system to help us set priorities for further information collection or special research. Once the system is large enough, it begins to be useful for the second main purpose: to help guide and promote direct conservation action. The data base could be used to help any individual to make more informed decisions. This could be a private landowner about to clear his or her "south forty"; it could be a conservationist trying to decide which lands to acquire or otherwise protect. It could be a developer seeking information about where to locate a new industrial plant. This kind of ongoing, continuously evolving, and increasingly powerful information system serves our ultimate aim—the confident and well-

Element (species) endangerment ranking factors.

1. Number of element occurrences
2. Total population size
3. Total range
4. Number of protected element occurrences
5. Relative ecological fragility
6. Relative degree of threat
7. Degree of legal protection
8. Taxonomic distinctness

Figure 1   *Endangerment ranking factors for species (elements).*

documented identification of those parts of the current landscape that are most important to the retention of endangered elements of our ecological diversity, and those most in need of aid at a given time.

Quite early in this inventory process we specifically highlight those plant and animal species believed to be in some peril. As we gather information on many species, we revise, correct, and rearrange these lists along a relative scale of endangerment. We use a formal "element ranking" system based on a standard set of factors or criteria to determine the rank of a particular species. The rank becomes our main basis for deciding how much further attention to give the species in both inventory and conservation efforts. Thus, we harness our energies on behalf of the nearly extinct at the expense of the demonstrably ineradicable.

Figure 1 lists our formal ranking factors. An "EO" is an "element occurrence"—for example, a single nest of a bald eagle. Of all the things that contribute to species endangerment, probably the most important is having few element occurrences. Consequently, element occurrence number is very high among the ranking considerations. Figure 2 shows an element ranking form for the Maryland darter. One of these forms is done on each

ELEMENT RANKING FORM

State: Md

Element Name: Etheostoma sellare

Date: 31 Aug. 1983

Common Name: Maryland darter

Prepared by: R.E. Jenkins, Jr.

Class: Animal - fish

Element Code: AFCQCØ268Ø

EO SPECIFICATIONS: Any stream reach containing a population

HABITAT OR COMMUNITY DESCRIPTION: Riffles in small streams

TAXONOMIC DISTINCTNESS: Good species in large genus.

PERMANENCE OF EO'S: Natural permanent. Fish occur in all seasons of the year.

FEDERAL STATUS: (LE) LT PE PT C1 C2 C AC N
Comments: Listed as endangered on 11 March 1967
in Federal Register 32 FR 4001

DEGREE OF LEGAL PROTECTION: Endangered Species act of 1973 provides certain protection.
Listed as state endangered under Md. nongame and Endangered Species Act on 17 July 1975,
providing added protection. 28 Aug. 1980, critical habitat proposed. Deer Creek. Desig-
RANKING CONSIDERATIONS   nated scenic river in 1973 (for other reasons) giving more
                              protection to habitat.

Estimated Total EO's: (A) B C D
Comments: Only known from a few riffles in 3 small streams (Swan, Gashey's Run Deer).
                              Since 1974 only seen in Deer Creek.

Estimated State EO's: (A) B C D (5 seen in '75, 2 in '77, 1 in '81)
Comments: Same as above

Total Range: (A1) A2 B C D
Comments: State endemic to Md., confined to Harford County.

Estimated adequately protected EO's in State: U (A) B C D
Comments: None completely protected

Relative Threat of Destruction: A (B) C D
Comments: Water quality could be degraded. Riffles could be silted in.

Ecological Fragility: A (B) C D
Comments: Presumed relatively resilient, but completely dependent on extremely limited
                              habitat.

State Range: (A) B C D
Comments: See total range comment.

OVERALL ELEMENT PRIORITY RANK: (A1) A2 AX B1 B2 B3 BU BX C D

Summarize reasons: Only occurs in one or two small populations on earth. Any more
endangered would be extinct.

NUMBER OF PROTECTED EO'S NEEDED IN STATE (include reasons) Complete protection of all
existing occurrences, at least as far as bufferage for the water sheds is feasible.

OTHER PROTECTION/STEWARDSHIP NEEDS: Need monitorage of existing populations, more information on life history, exploration of potential for transplantation and captive culture.

Figure 2 *Element ranking form for the Maryland darter*

species that we deal with in a given state. This particular darter is ranked as highly as we rank any species. We give it an A-1; it has a very narrow range, being endemic to a few riffles in two small streams. It really could not be much rarer and still persist—in fact, there is some doubt whether it still does persist. Note that the information used is not complete, but it is more than adequate to document the extreme endangerment of this species.

Let us consider a case further down our endangerment continuum, the tiger salamander. When we looked at the data on this species using the same biological, distributional, and locational variables, we found that it ranked well down the line, in Category C. It turns out that the tiger salamander is one of the more widespread and abundant amphibians in the United States. It comes close to being in the D Category of relative endangerment at the "ineradicable" end of the scale. Nevertheless, this species was rather widely urged upon us by various herpetologists as deserving priority attention. Had we proceeded solely on the basis of widespread enthusiasm, we would now be busy misallocating our scarce resources.

Figure 3 is a sample of what we call a "natural diversity scorecard" for a given state. This particular one is for animals; there are separate scorecards for the special plants, special animals, and communities in each state. This scorecard summarizes four kinds of data. First, the elements are displayed in descending order of endangerment; these are the driving factors of the scorecard. Second, the scorecard displays occurrences or locations where the elements in question can be found. These occurrences are ranked by their quality, condition, viability, and defensibility. Third, we have data on sites that are potential preserves designed to capture one or more element occurrences in an ecologically sustainable unit. Fourth, we have the land ownership tracts that are combined to form a potential preserve or site. All of the individual tracts composing a site must be protected or only an inviable or indefensible preserve fragment will be established. For each tract of the potential site assemblage, we append information on the current and intended protective status. The discrepancies between the two constitute our land-conservation agenda.

Now we could have a long debate about whether the kind of preserves that these scorecards call for are adequate. We are talking about microdot remnants of ecosystems in many cases. Island biogeographic theory seems to suggest that Yellowstone National Park, for example, is "too small" as a preserve "island" to sustain a great many of its species over the next thousand years at projected rates of "species relaxation." Time will tell whether this proposition is valid, but it is not very helpful in making today's decisions. We are not planning for a thousand years or five-hundred years. We are planning for what can sustain the last populations of plant and animal species this year, next year, and the year after. What we are calling a "viable" and "defensible" preserve for some of these species is not in all instances going to sustain them forever. These preserves are lifeboats, and one does not plan to live forever on a lifeboat; they are intended to get us through an immediate emergency. In the same way, most of the micro-reserves that we can realistically establish today are not expected to be successful "planets" for ecological continuance over millennia. In some instances, they may suffice; for certain kinds of organisms in certain circumstances, even these relatively small pieces of property may perpetuate them indefinitely. For the rest, these small preserves are selected and designed as well as we know how to sustain the target species through an immediate crisis. We hope that eventually opportunities will arise for such organisms to reoccupy a larger area.

We will now consider some examples. You will notice that one of the most endangered animal species on the natural diversity scorecard in Figure 3 is the Indiana bat (*Myotis sodalis*). An important locality for this species is Barnett Cave in Foster's Woods, Tennessee. As is usual, the bat is not the only interesting organism found there. The woods also contain a population of *Spiranthes ovalis*, a regionally rare Lady's Tress Orchid. Of even greater importance in this assemblege is a population of Price's potato bean (*Apios priceana*), which is one of the few endangered plants recognized as such on the federal list. Our element ranking sheet on that species would show that it is known currently only from 13 populations, scattered through 5 different states.

These several imperiled species, along with some others of lesser interest, co-occur on an area of only 16 hectares (40 acres) in northern Tennessee, which we have decided should constitute a preserve. This micro-preserve does not remind us of Yellowstone, but it has been selected carefully and designed to provide for the populations in question. It probably cannot be improved materially for this purpose. The 40 acres include not just the plant populations and cave entrance but surrounding buff-erage designed to limit encroachment from off-site effects. Over this ecological boundary, we superimposed the actual property ownership lines on our preserve plan, which brings us to the bottom line—protecting the land.

To do this, we have to protect each of the properties falling within our proposed boundaries. We can do this by outright land acquisition, by acquiring partial rights such as a conservation easement, or by convincing

STATE NATURAL DIVERSITY SCORECARD -- VERTEBRATES -- INDIANA

ELEMENT NAME and CODE	ELEMENT RANK	EO#	EO RANK	SITE NAME and CODE
Myotis sodalis	A2	018	A	Big Dome
(Indiana bat)		012	A	Windy Cave
FD498		004	A	Bill's Cave
		017	A	Bat Cave
			A	Iroquois Cave
			B	Raccoon Cave
Natrix erythragaster neglecta	B2	016	A	Duck Pond Cypress S
(Copperbelly water snake)		019	A-B	
00665				Hollow Bottoms
			B	Muscatatuck N.W.Ref
				(see Accipiter
Cyptobranchus alleganiensis	B2	005	A-B	Blue River Populatic
(Hellbender)				
Sorex Hoyi	B3	001		Harrison Crawford S
(Pygmy shrew)				
FA4B7				
Sorex fumeus	B3	001	A	Harrison Crawford
(Smokey shrew)				
FA514				
Neotoma floridana	B3		B	Close Curve Farm
(Eastern woodrat)			B	Neotoma #1
FL500				
Sylvilagus aquaticus	B3			Duck Pond Cypress S
(Swamp rabbit)				
FF518				
"				
"				
(continued)				

1. EO=Element occurrences. Ranks A-D stand for excellent, good, marginal defensibility.

2. CS and IS=Current status and intended status. Numbers indicate increa (conservation ownerships and legal dedication.

Figure 3   *State natural diversity scorecard for vertebrates in Indiana.*

TRACT CODE	TRACT OWNER	CS	IS	COMMENTS
a	IND Div Forestry	9	9	100K bats, 2nd best EO, fence
a	Jackson	2	7	3.5K bats, gift easement, TNC +
a		1	7	Try for easemt. gate, mon
a	IND Div Forestry	1	9	50K pop, 5th best EO, DNP to acq
a	IDF	1	6	Regulate visit in winter
	Jackson	0	2	Nominate

e Bald Cypress slough, <u>Sylvilagus</u>)

TRACT CODE	TRACT OWNER	CS	IS	COMMENTS
a	Hardy	2	2	
b	Jenkins	1	8	to Evansvill Audubon Soc.
c	Morse	2	8	
d	Lukowski	2	2	
a	US F & W	2	2	Encourage specific EO mgmt.
a	IND Div Forestry	0	2	Notify, no immediate threat.
	IND Div Forestry	1	3	Try for MA pending field work
	IND Div Forestry	1	3	
		2	2	prevent cutting
a	Johns	1	3	prevent cutting

e Bald Cypress Slough, <u>Natrix</u>)

r on the basis of overall quality, condition, viability, and

ength of protection for each tract from 0 (absolutely no protection) to 9

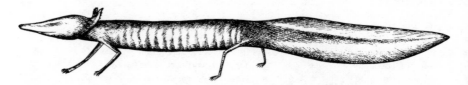

Figure 4   *The Texas blind salamander* (Typhlomolge rathbuni) *has very slender limbs and rudimentary eyes covered by skin. Due to environmental changes in its habitat, the species is now endangered. Illustration by Vichai Malikul.*

the existing landowners to take care of these properties in a way that will prevent their biological destruction.

ALTERNATIVES IN LAND CONSERVATION

The Nature Conservancy is best known for its activities in acquiring land, having acquired outright 800,000 hectares (2-million acres) over the last 30 years. However, land acquisition is not always possible, nor is it always the most effective way to allocate limited funds to protect land. In some instances, it may be better to secure a conservation easement under which the easement holder does not take possession of the property but instead secures certain specified negative rights in land. The fee owner is then able to continue agreed-upon acceptable land uses but waives certain rights, for example, to harvest timber or plow prairies.

Sometimes the land in need of protection already belongs to a public agency but is not adequately protected or correctly managed. In such cases, nearly all agencies have a number of administrative categories to which such an area can be designated so as to ensure particularly careful management or protection.

Another nonacquisition device is simple notification of a private or public landowner that something on his or her property is of importance. This prevents accidental destruction, and in many instances the landowner will care for a resource once its significance is known. Such a landowner may be willing to go further and enter into a registration agreement, which basically constitutes an "administrative" promise to continue appropriate ecological management.

These sorts of protection alternatives are becoming increasingly important to the conservancy for a couple of reasons. One is that they make our resources go farther. We may be able to protect sufficiently larger pieces of our natural biological estate with these tools than we could through outright fair-market purchase. The other reason is that within a typical multitract assemblage it is rare that all the owners are interested in giving up their property. When faced with this situation, acquiring only the parcels owned by willing conveyors may only protect an inviable and indefensible mosaic. We need to have the whole spectrum of protection tools at our disposal. We find some owners who would like to sell and others who might be willing to donate their property (partly for the tax deduction). Some might be willing to register their property and promise to manage it wisely; others may be willing to sell or give an easement. Some might be willing to convey a right of first refusal, giving the conservancy a legal right to match any other offer should the owner decide to sell. Of course, some people may not wish to make any commitment. For these hard cases, we just have to be patient and keep after them.

MANAGEMENT AND RESTORATION TECHNIQUES

If an organization protects land through some form of acquisition, it must also manage it. The Nature Conservancy now owns about 700 preserves totaling more than 200,000 hectares (500,000 acres) scattered all across the country. These range in size from more than 20,000 hectares (50,000 acres) down to less than 1 acre and vary widely in the reasons for their preservation.

To manage such a system of preserves effectively requires careful planning and an organized combination of staff and volunteers. We try to organize our land stewardship efforts along the same lines as for protection; we target our energies on those species and ecosystems that are more endangered, that require intervention to maintain themselves, and that can benefit from our active mangement. For the rest, we carry out ordinary maintenance and care, but our rule is "If it ain't broke, don't fix it." Thus, we are spared the misallocation of scarce resources entailed in willy-nilly land management in which "hobbysim" reigns and first things are not put first.

We thus focus most of our resources on maintaining the less stable ecosystem components of our preserves and the most sensitive species. Management practices range from simple techniques, such as routing trails away from rare and fragile plant populations, to major interventions such as managed burnings. In the most extreme cases, we go even further, attempting to repair damaged ecosystems or restore those that have been completely altered.

As with many other land-management agencies, fire has become an important ingredient in conservancy practices. Many of our native ecosystems were adapted to periodic ground fires, and, under today's conditions of fragmented landscapes and extensive fire suppression, it is often necessary to start controlled fires to burn-off choking ground litter, to reduce accumulating fuels that support destructive conflagration fires, and to suppress certain intrusive exotics or invaders. Such prescribed burns are appropriate not only in prairies and grasslands but in southeastern pine woods, certain northwestern forests, and southwestern chaparral.

Our stewardship planning not only leads to more efficient allocation of direct management efforts but frequently reveals critical research needs that would otherwise have been lost in the shuffle. Careful setting of priorities not only pinpoints such research needs but frees up time from less important tasks to pursue them. For some of our most endangered U.S. plant species, this orderly process is allowing us to coordinate the efforts of conservancy units throughout their ranges to monitor populations, correlate population trends with ecological variables, bring field observations together with laboratory experiments, and, from all of this, to develop solid guidelines for management, propagation, or whatever is needed.

Some of our management interventions are certainly artificial, but they are intended, paradoxically, to achieve a more "natural" result than would occur if the situation were left alone to deteriorate. There is the case, for example, of the Gila Chub (*Gila intermedia*). This animal occurs with several other endangered southwestern fish at a place called the Canelo Hill Cienega, a desert spring wetland in southern Arizona. The wetland also has one of only four known populations of a rare Lady's Tress Orchid (*Spiranthes gramina*). Just as we were acquiring the first tract of this preserve a number of years ago, down-cutting channel erosion of the outlet stream reached the point where the wetland suddenly began to drain away. To maintain the rare ecosystem, we decided to build a dam (a blatantly "nonnatural" intervention, but it replaced a preexisting natural dam). Few cienegas remain as habitats for these special organisms, so it is imperative to preserve them when and how we can.

Another case involves a pristine section of the South Platte River in central Nebraska, a great staging ground for the sandhill and endangered whooping cranes. In its pristine state, the South Platte formerly had a low gradient, braided river channel. Frequent natural spring floods carried along winter ice floes that scoured out the woody growth and maintained meadowlands and bare sand bars ideally suited for feeding and resting cranes. The construction of upstream impoundments has curtailed these natural floods to the point that encroaching woody growth is making the habitat unsuitable for the cranes. Fire provides one corrective remedy for periodically reducing the woody growth and encouraging the growth of meadowlands. One of our cooperators, the Whooping Crane Trust, goes even further by employing a giant piece of specially designed machinery to shred encroaching shrubs and small trees. Both whooping and sandhill cranes now use artificially maintained areas.

Ezell's Cave in central Texas is a wonderful example of the assemblages of organisms that can exist mysteriously, almost out of our sight. The cave was registered as one of the first National Natural Landmarks because it contains one of the richest troglodytic (cave-dwelling) faunas in the United States. More than 200 species of organisms are found in this cave, many of which are aquatic denizens of the aquifer underlying the Edwards Plateau. This cave happens to be a window into that particular subterranean system. Ezell's Cave is the only place where we can reliably encounter the unique Texas blind salamander (*Typhlomolge rathbuni*, Figure 4). Besides this, the cave contains a *Palaemonetes* shrimp, which is known from only one other cave in the world; a flat worm, known from only two other caves; a shrimp-like crustacean, *Mesocyclops*, known from only this cave and another in Asia; a *Monodella* shrimp; and at least one other crustacean known from nowhere else.

When The Nature Conservancy acquired the property, the vertical cave entrance had been sealed with cement to protect against accident liability. This had eliminated a Mexican freetail bat colony that used to roost during part of the year over the first pool in the cave. At the time, bat guano was thought to be the basic energy source for the whole cave ecosystem. After we acquired the cave, we intervened in several ways. We removed the concrete seal and replaced it with a cave grate—but the bats did not return. We replaced the grate with a chainlink fence—but the bats still did not return. Three separate attempts, employing various techniques, to reintroduce bats all failed. The good news is that in spite of past impacts, the system seems to be operating successfully, with stable populations of the key species still surviving. Apparently, sufficient nutrients are entering the groundwater system elsewhere.

As this case shows, intervening in natural processes is a chancy undertaking. What we intend is often not what happens. Therefore, we prefer overlarge preserves where natural conditions can predominate and where species can get along perfectly well without clumsy attempts at assistance by us. This would be what Dr. Seal called a "safe-fail" situation, but as our remaining natural landscapes are broken up, wholly adequate biological reserves are increasingly hard to establish. As our biotic lifeboats shrink, we expect the necessity for intervention to become more and more frequent.

Thus far, the cases mentioned involve relatively coarse approaches to biological management. These may suffice when a system is only slightly disrupted or when only a few species require direct attention. In seriously disrupted systems, especially when these are last remnants of particular habitats, intervention may need to be much more intensive. Where we have attempted to restore systems, we have done so not only for the direct results but also to gain expertise in restoration techniques. We anticipate that in spite of all the best efforts at conservation, the condition of many of our biological habitats is going to worsen. As the need for intervention and outright restoration increases, we hope to develop sufficient knowledge to be able to do what is required.

Over the years, we have undertaken or cooperated on a number of restoration projects all over the country, mainly in systems, such as marshes and prairies, dominated by herbaceous plants. We have been involved in a number of projects in some forest and woodland situations as well. Our most ambitious effort began in 1972 when we established the Center for Applied Research in Environmental Sciences (now called Environmental Concern, Inc.) to attempt to restore salt marshes. Such marshes are relatively simple systems dominated by a small number of primary producers with short life cycles. Therefore, they are good systems upon which to experiment. The center's staff gathered salt-marsh seeds from nearly 20 species and got them to germinate under artifical lights. They raised the plants to larger sizes in greenhouses and irrigated nurseries with salt water before transplanting them to the field. They barged tons of sand to create the necessary substrate at our main research site in the Chesapeake Bay. They contrived artifical breakwaters that would reduce water energy levels to keep the shelving substrate from eroding before our transplants could get a firm footing and stabilize the situation.

Nature does not seem to help in some of these restoration projects. Big bare patches developed where the Canada geese and blue crabs ate the *Spartina* grass rhizomes. Some plants failed, and the composition took on unintended (but presumably better-adapted) patterns. Eventually, we succeeded in establishing several salt marshes that resembled natural marshes in most respects. Time will tell whether these marshes become successful and stable ecosystems, evolve into something different, or eventually disappear.

It is too bad that current circumstances force conservation to such difficult and uncertain initiatives, but we seem to have no choice if we are to prevent the elimination of entire ecosystem types and habitats. Perhaps some day, with the arrival of the millenium, we will get past this era of man-induced environmental crunch to a time when nature can once again take care of itself. Meanwhile, with every escalation in ecological stress we feel called upon to compensate with a whole panoply of increasingly sophisticated and complex conservation technology tools. I hope that we can keep up in this deadly serious race.

10

The Realities Of Reintroducing Species To The Wild

EUGENE S. MORTON

One might think that reintroducing species to the wild is a rather simple topic, but I will try to make clear that it is not a proven technique by which to ensure the survival of species within natural habitats. We will look at some of the complexities reintroduction entails and see how reintroduction is also a way to study animals that presents us with unique opportunities to learn more about them. We will also examine the unforeseen effects of altering habitats, even when the alterations are not of the "bulldozer" type.

This presentation will focus on tropical ecosystems, especially the New World tropics or Neotropics, because this is where I have done most of my work. However, I want to emphasize that the Neotropics does not represent an exotic, faraway land, especially when birds are considered. Up to 80 percent of the birds we see and take for granted in the forests of the eastern United States head south every fall to Neotropic areas where they will spend up to nine months of the year, more time than they spend here in their breeding areas. One can see them moving in the daytime; one can literally hear them at night. The forest destruction discussed extensively in this symposium affects us in many ways, one effect being on the migrant birds that we take for granted as "our" birds. More can be read about this topic in recent articles in *Defenders of Wildlife* (Lovejoy 1981), *Natural History* (Fitzpatrick 1982), and the *Smithsonian Magazine* (Pasquier and Morton 1982).

Reintroducing species is a much more complex problem than the mere mechanics of the process might suggest. These problems underscore the approaches or philosophies of today's avian ecologists. Unlike those ecologists who study large mammals or primates, and particularly those who study adaptations of individual animals within a social group, ornithologists tend to assume that "a bird is a bird" and can be studied on the species level rather than on the individual or population level. The study of avian communities, as it is called in ecology, therefore tends to lead us away from studying those adaptations of individuals with which we should be concerned. This is very limiting because if we try to reintroduce a species, what we are actually doing is putting back individuals of that species into the wild. Such reintroduction attempts force us to study the adaptive nature of individuals in relation to their habitat. We cannot describe or foresee what certain alterations of the habitat will produce (in terms of successful reintroductions) without first knowing what adaptations the animals already have made to their habitat—including learned behaviors— and what specific attributes of the animals' habitat are limiting. I would like to discuss a very specific example.

First, we will consider some general aspects of the reintroduction of birds. John Long has written a book, *Introduced Birds of the World* (1981), in which he tabulates successful attempts to introduce birds since the early 1800s. The book is probably the most extensive compendium on this subject for any animal group. Long documents 1,197 introductions, including exotic species (that is, species foreign to the area into which they were introduced) as well as relocations or reintroductions of native species into those areas from which they previously had been extirpated. Worldwide, 576 of these attempts failed, constituting 48 percent of the total. In North America, 53 percent of the attempted introductions and reintroductions failed. This is interesting because it means the chances of success for introducing or reintroducing birds is about like the toss of a coin. Not too much predictive power there! If we look at just those species that were reintroduced into an area once native for them, the success rate is 52 percent— another flip of the coin. However, if we look at just the exotic species, the success rate is only 29 percent—a more predictable result. Clearly, it is even more difficult to introduce a species into a totally new area than it is to reintroduce a species into an area where it once lived but does so no longer. Nevertheless, in either case success rates are poor. That is why the actual experience of these attempts has not been studied from a theoretical level.

Second, I will discuss a reintroduction study I did on Barro Colorado Island (BCI) in Panama (Figure 1). BCI is roughly circular and about 15 square kilometers (6 mi²) in area. It was formed when Gatun Lake and

Figure 1 Map of the Panama Canal Zone and Barro Colorado Island (BCI) situated within it. Illustration by Kathleen Spagnola.

the Panama Canal were dug in 1913. Originally, BCI was a hilltop surrounded by forest. Although it is an island, keep in mind that it still is, in effect, a hilltop. Since 1923, it has been protected from legal hunting and has been studied extensively. The Smithsonian Tropical Research Institute maintains it to this day. Fortunately, several people, notably Ed Willis and Eugene Eisenmann (1979), have completed long-term studies of bird populations on the island. They found that between 1960 and 1971, 42 species of birds were extirpated on BCI (Willis, 1974a, b). Of these, most were lost due to the maturing of the island's forests; some species characteristic of successional, young forests and fields simply died out because after awhile there was no habitat left. But at least 14 species seemed to have died out for "nonsuccessional" reasons. These were forest birds which had plenty of natural habitat on BCI. The only theory offered to explain this die-off—the "island biogeographic theory"—was prevalent at the time. This theory suggested that the size of the island would of itself cause a number of species to become extinct; that one could predict within a certain variance how many species might be lost from Barro Colorado after it became an island simply by knowing the size of the island. This theory, however, did not explain what actually had occurred.

I wanted to know the direct causes of extirpation for at least some of these 14 species because I wanted to explore the feasibility of reintroducing species to forest preserves in the tropics. As time goes on, such reintroductions are going to be more and more necessary because when fragmented sections of tropical forests are preserved, they become, in effect, habitat "islands" surrounded by deforested agricultural land.

Two of the fourteen species extirpated were wrens. Because I had already been studying wrens, I decided to reintroduce two species, the song wren (*Cyphorhinus phaeocephalus*) and the white-breasted wood wren (*Henicorhina leucosticta*), on BCI. These two species were common in mainland forests near BCI but apparently would not cross even a small, 300-meter watergap to recolonize the island. Where they did occur, these wrens were quite conspicuous because of their noise. Compared with temperate zone birds, however, they were actually rather rare. As mentioned earlier in this symposium, rarity itself can make extinction more likely to occur, but rarity does not necessarily indicate that a process of extinction has begun. In this case, it must be emphasized that these wrens were properly considered "common" by ornithologists who work in the tropics because they did occur at normal density and had not become rare due to habitat alteration. We could say that they were naturally rare. Rarity in itself can produce a syndrome of adaptations, especially those that have to do with

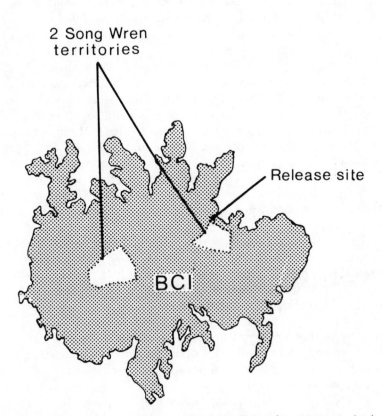

2 Song Wren
territories

Release site

BCI

Figure 2   *Map of Barro Colorado Island with release site and song wren territories depicted. Illustration by Kathleen Spagnola.*

escaping from predators. Such adaptations have evolved in a large number of tropical species of birds and other organisms. The wrens were typical in other ways as well: they were insectivorous, and their social systems were of the most common type. They, and about 60 percent of all the perching birds in Panama, have permanent year-long pair bonds and permanent territories. I thought that their sedentary habit might facilitate a reintroduction. Presumably, they would not quickly fly away, but that remained to be seen.

I captured seven individuals of each of the two wren species from the wild on the mainland and immediately carried them back to Barro Colorado Island where they were all released from the same location. I did not expect this reintroduction to be successful—that is, I did not expect that the birds would reproduce and become once again a normal part of the avifauna of BCI. They had been extirpated there once and probably would be again. I wanted to find out what had caused their demise, so that when they again became extinct they could show me why in the process. This type of information could be helpful in attempts to reintroduce captive-raised birds.

The wrens were released in June 1976, and I checked on them again in December of 1976, through the following May, and then every October until 1980 when all but one of them apparently had died off. When I first checked them in December 1976, I had many hypotheses to test concerning the fact that no territorial or social pressure would be put on them from other wrens. It seemed that they would settle in the best habitats available because of this absence of pressure. Other questions were: Would pairs break up and reform easily, and would the birds' social system affect their ability to find one another and possibly reduce effectiveness when permanently pair-bonded birds were reintroduced? This turned out to create no difficulty, as the birds generally formed into new pairs. I knew which birds were already mated when I caught them because I had put color bands on their legs.

In December 1976, I found that one new pair of song wrens consisted of the male of one pair and the female of another. They had swapped mates and were living 2,000 meters apart. One pair was right at the top of the island and another pair right near the release point (Figure 2). Not only had they reformed pairs, but they had each successfully fledged clutches, which consist of two young in song wrens, a family group size common in many other species in the tropics. A bird that was extirpated on the island had, therefore, not only managed to survive well but had also reproduced—a sure sign that this reintroduction was successful. The birds seemed to be doing splendidly. At the time, I could not figure out why the birds had settled so far apart, for there was intervening forest habitat that seemed to me to be equally capable of supporting them.

One hypothesis that I tested, which derived from competition theory, was that the song wrens would choose territories where potential competitors, in this case antwrens, were least common. Since the original demise of the wrens on BCI, these antwrens had become four times more common there than on the nearby mainland. One could encounter a flock of antwrens about every 200 meters along the trails on BCI, whereas on the mainland one met them about every 1,000 meters. I thought that, due to their abundance on BCI, the antwrens might be competitors of the wrens and cause their extinction. However, this was not the case. I found that the wrens had settled in locations bearing no relationship to the density of antwrens.

The white-breasted wood wrens had chosen habitat that was, in fact, not forest but little patches of second growth left on the island's shoreline and in large tree falls. I concluded that the earlier loss of that species was probably due to loss of habitat as the island's forests matured. This demise was, afterall, not a "nonsuccessional" loss as had been suggested earlier. In contrast, the song wrens settled in forest habitat, and they weighed as much or more after they were reestablished on BCI than when I had captured them. This ruled out any problem of obtaining food. The possible causes of their earlier extirpation gradually narrowed. I finally became convinced that song wrens became extinct on Barro Colorado because of the type of nest they built and where they placed it.

I had found the nests of the first two song wren pairs that had been successful in fledging young (Figure 3). These nests were placed near the most sluggish streams on the island. Remember that BCI is a hilltop. Both nests were in the same species of sapling tree and were placed at eye level. The nests incorporated a heap of leaves and mimicked what a bunch of flotsam at high water would look like if it were caught in a tree branch near a stream that periodically rises and falls. When the stream falls, such clumps of detritus are abundant along its course.

The song wren not only uses its well-camouflaged nest for breeding but also spends every night there; these nests are dormitories as well. The family groups go back to the nests every evening and settle down for the night. It is probably safer to stay in your nest, especially if you are rare, because of the many predators. If your nest itself is rare relative to the detritus piles that it mimics, it can be an effective ruse for survival. Unfortunately, because BCI is a hilltop it has very few streams that are sluggish and slow-moving. In fact, it has none that rise and fall to the extent that

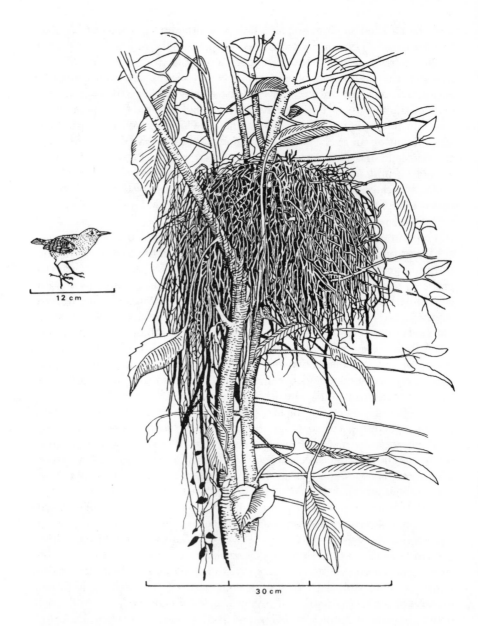

12 cm

30 cm

Figure 3   *The song wren* (Cyporhinus phaeocephalus) *and its nest. Illustration by Kathleen Spagnola.*

lowland streams do. The first two song wren nests were probably successful, I surmise, because they were placed along streams. As soon as the
nests were discovered by predators, the birds were frightened out of them
at night and looked elsewhere for new nest placements. Surprisingly, all of
the subsequent nests we found were along trails (Figure 4). Why? The
trails apparently looked to the birds like streams, and, in fact, some BCI
trails do carry water during heavy rains. Consequently, I suggest that the
slight habitat alteration on BCI caused by miles of trails could have led to
the demise of the song wrens. Their demise might have occurred anyway
simply because of the absence of sluggish streams beside which the cam-
ouflaged nests could go undetected. Today only a single song wren remains on BCI, and lone birds do not build dormitories.

This brings us back to the question of a species' critical adaptations and
the specific attributes of a habitat that may be limiting for it. In the case of
the song wren, a critical element in the wren's life cycle was the permanent
dormitory nest, a nest that mimics detritus and must be realistically located. Once the nests placed by streams were discovered, few places were
left on BCI for the wrens to go to other than the trails, which were heavily
used by coatis and other predators. On these trails, new nests were discovered even more rapidly than the original ones. On Barro Colorado, the essential ploy could not work. The song wrens found on BCI before it became an island were probably birds that had been forced out of their good
habitat as the lake formed. As Dr. Lovejoy mentioned earlier with regard
to forest fragmentation, an influx of birds probably occurred, and the birds
had to go somewhere, so they ended up on Barro Colorado. They made it
for a few years but could not survive permanently.

The song wren, whose demise I believe I have pinpointed, shows that
while island biogeographic theory may predict overall numbers of species
that may become extinct, it does not reveal the underlying causes of extinction for any one species. These causes can and must be identified before
reintroduction should be attempted. The song wrens also illustrate the importance of learned behaviors, which for many species probably cannot be
maintained in captive populations whose progeny might be considered for
reintroduction to the wild.

The "cultural inheritance" that the wild birds had when I released them
consisted of many things besides placing their special nests in an appropriate habitat. Their foraging behavior probably was at least partly learned
and would almost certainly be lost in captive birds. They forage close together on the forest floor in leaf litter, so that when one bird scares a katy-
did or a cockroach from a leaf it has just looked under, the adjacent bird

Figure 4 *A song wren's nest erroneously placed along a BCI trail. Illustration by Kathleen Spagnola.*

can capture it. This way they flush insects to one another in a group operation. How could one maintain this habit in captive animals that are fed a controlled diet from a food pan? To be completely honest, the probability of maintaining all the avifauna in a forest "island" preserve through reintroductions of species is extremely low. It is just not feasible. Introducing particular species carefully chosen in advance for intensive research is feasible, but it would be an arrogant assumption on the part of humans to believe that they can maintain, through captive breeding, entire functioning communities, entire ecosystems. Surely the best answer is to maintain throughout the world habitats of adequate size and diversity so that nature can take care of itself.

References Cited and Additional Readings

Fitzpatrick, J. W.
1982.   Northern birds at home in the tropics. *Natural History* 91: 40–47.

Long, J. L.
1981.   *Introduced Birds of the World: The Worldwide History, Distribution and Influence of Birds Introduced to New Environments.* New York: Universe Books.

Lovejoy, T. E.
1981.   Fading tropical forests. *Defenders* 56:2–5.

Pasquier, R. F. and E. S. Morton.
1982.   Why birds take winter vacations. *Smithsonian* 13:169.

Willis, E. O.
1974a.   Populations and local extinctions of birds on Barro Colorado Island, Panama. *Smithsonian Contributions to Zoology* 291:1–31.

1974b.   Populations and local extinctions of birds on Barro Colorado Island, Panama. *Ecological Monographs* 44:153–69.

Willis, E. O. and E. Eisenmann.
1979.   A revised list of birds of Barro Colorado Island, Panama. *Smithsonian Contributions to Zoology* 291:1–31.

11

Extinctions And Ecosystem Functions:

Implications For Humankind

P A U L   R.   E H R L I C H

I am not going to be the bearer of good news. I will focus on exactly the topic that was announced, so therefore I will present some grim facts about how extinctions are going to affect and already are affecting the functioning of ecological systems, and what this will mean to us and others. By ecological system, or ecosystem, I mean the interrelated community of organisms that lives in an area: the plants, animals, and microorganisms that are combined into a system with their physical environment.

I do not want to begin, however, without expressing that I think almost all the people attending this symposium, and almost all biologists, have important ethical, aesthetic, and compassionate concerns about this subject that go beyond the impact that extinctions will have on their own lives. And I believe that while businessmen and others with less-direct concern for the natural world can, perhaps, be persuaded to action by arguments about economic and other benefits to human beings, we must, if we are going to solve this problem in any permanent way, create a feeling for other organisms that goes beyond what they might or might not do for *Homo sapiens*. In this I agree with David Ehrenfeld, the author of an excellent book, *The Arrogance of Humanism* (1978). Fostering the sort of concern that goes beyond self-interest and self-preservation is one of the things that is done so well by Washington's National Zoo.

Those who know the literature of ecology know that we do not understand ecosystems very well; they are tremendously complex, as are human social systems. Therefore, I also must add a caveat: that although we do know a few things, we need to rely heavily on predictions derived from basic principles. The experiment on ecosystem decay in fragmented forests that Dr. Lovejoy described in his presentation is magnificent, but the logistics of conducting such experiments are extremely difficult. Much of what I am going to describe is the result of work that Dr. Harold Mooney and I have been doing jointly at Stanford (Ehrlich and Mooney, 1983), and much of it is highly speculative. One can criticize it severely on those grounds, as some people have done. However, as I think this symposium demonstrates, if we do nothing until we are absolutely sure about what the effects of extinctions are going to be in ecosystem functioning, about what the actual size of a preserve has to be—down to the nearest tenth of a kilometer—before we establish one, we will not have to worry about the problem at all. We do not have the luxury of waiting until all the proof is in because the problem is overwhelming us at a much more rapid rate than the proof is arriving.

I think some things are almost self-evident today. We are exhausting the nonrenewable resources of our planet relatively rapidly. This is automatically pushing us more and more into dependence on "flow" resources such as timber, fibers, and energy from various forms of biomass. As a result, more and more pressure is put on our ecosystems to directly supply goods and services that humanity needs to support an apparently ever-growing human population.

Few people in our society, and certainly few of our decision makers, understand that the ecological systems of the planet provide *Homo sapiens* with a whole series of little recognized but absolutely essential services, without which civilization cannot exist—indeed, without which *Homo sapiens* cannot exist. Just briefly, let me go over a few of the services provided by a number of different organisms, including some that are quite obscure to lay people such as bacteria and mycorrhizal fungi. One is maintenance of the quality of the atmosphere. It is nice to breathe a mixture of nitrogen and oxygen in the right proportions, and it is useful not to have a lot of ammonia in it.

It is well known that the plants of our planet play a very large role in shaping the climate by changing the albedo—the reflectivity of the planet—and by recycling water. Nonwoody plants stand upright because they are continually transpiring water. The leaves of woody plants look awfully funny if they are not transpiring water, as anyone who has ever potted one at home and then gone away for a three-week vacation has learned.

Moreover, the ecosystems of this planet generate and preserve our soils. They are not doing such a good job anymore because of the many substitutions human beings have made in ecosystems. As Lester Brown (1980) has recently written, humanity can perhaps survive the depletion of nonrenewable supplies of fossil fuels, but it certainly cannot survive the current rate of soil depletion. Natural ecological systems also recycle the nutrients that are essential not only to the ecosystems themselves but also to agriculture.

Natural ecosystems provide us with food from the sea. True, the availability of such food has plateaued due to a combination of overexploitation and pollution. Nonetheless, the 70- to 80-million metric tons of fish that come out of the sea annually are a critical portion of humanity's diet, particularly for the poorer segments of humanity.

The vast majority, well over 97 percent and possibly more than 99 percent, of potential crop pests and vectors of human disease are controlled by natural ecological systems. Finally, natural ecosystems maintain a "genetic library" from which humanity has already withdrawn the very basis of its civilization in terms of food, drugs, and industrial products. The potential of this genetic library for further withdrawals of enormous value to mankind is well known; it is at least equivalent to or perhaps an order of magnitude greater than what has already been removed.

The critical point to remember is that millions of species and billions of genetically distinct natural populations on this planet are essential working parts of the ecosystems that provide humanity with the services just described. At the same time, we must realize that humanity is currently launching an all-out assault on these very systems. That assault is causing an epidemic of extinctions, which, in my view, is massively underestimated in typical discussions. This is because, first, those discussions usually are about the coming disappearance of well-recognized, large organisms and, second, they emphasize the disappearance of species rather than of populations. We all recognize that people like and appreciate large animals for a variety of reasons, but in general they do not have so important a function in supplying ecosystem services as do small organisms such as insects, some obscure plants, and bacteria. I am talking about the contrast between a cheetah and a pollinating bee, for instance. Also, considered solely from the point of view of ecosystem functioning, the loss of a spectacular species is usually not of the most grave concern. Take, for example, the highly endangered California condor, a wonderful bird that for many reasons we want to preserve. True, the condor is a decomposer (a carrion feeder), but decomposition in California would not go on at a significantly lower rate if the last 30 California condors were exterminated. Just as an aside, I might point out that by the time something appears on the U.S. Endangered Species List, it might as well already be gone from the point of view of ecosystem functioning.

With regard to ecosystem functioning, we must be deeply concerned about the continual destruction of local populations, which is going on at an enormously high rate—much higher than that of the loss of species. Every time a large chunk of hitherto undisturbed land is destroyed, we are losing not only many populations but probably also several species of obscure organisms that have not yet been even catalogued by *Homo sapiens*. In many cases, these organisms' role in the ecosystem is not yet understood. So we are in the middle of an epidemic of extinctions—not just extinctions of species but extinctions of local populations. These populations are all working parts of ecological systems.

This raises two critical questions: first, what can be predicted about the impact of the extinction of a single population or species upon the delivery of ecosystem services? And second, to what degree can these populations or species be substituted for in terms of the delivery of ecosystem services?

This second question is the one that Dr. Mooney and I have concentrated on the most. In other words, if we eliminate population "A" and thereby lose a portion of or an entire ecosystem service, is there some way to restore the service, either by reintroducing organisms into that ecosystem from another population of the same species or from a different species or by substituting, instead, human artifacts? An example of the latter could be, for instance, trying to restore flood control services lost through deforestation by putting in a dam. The question is whether society can make substitutions for these ecosystem service impairments and restore the service to its previous level.

These are crucial questions in the political sphere because a number of economists in the world—having never had the slightest contact with how the natural world works—are under the impression that we can substitute indefinitely for any lost resource. Many people have seen in a recent "April Fool" issue of *Science* magazine (curiously published in June!) an article by Julian Simon (1980), in which he announced that, among other things, humanity did not have to worry about the supply of copper because copper can be made from other metals. He suggested that the only theoretical limit on the amount of copper that could be made available to humanity is the "weight of the universe!" This is the so-called "cornucopian" school of economics.

I recently went rafting down a river with a good friend who is an economist. He does not hold any of these views, but he always likes to joke about economists. When we could not find a can opener, he said, "Why don't we take the economists' solution for this?" I asked, "What's that?" He said, "Let us assume a can opener." Cornucopians assume there are no laws of nature; that large-scale alchemy is feasible.

Quite seriously, though, many economists and others think that society can just continuously substitute for any resources it has used up. This is also a common economic approach to biological resources: after one stock of fishes is exterminated, another stock of fishes to exterminate can always be found. This is their belief, quite literally. I was told by a Japanese news-paperman how the Japanese economists justify the continual wiping out of whale stocks by the whaling industry. I had said that I could not under-stand why the whaling industry would want to drive itself to extinction. He said, "You are thinking of the whaling industry as an organization that is interested in maintaining whales; actually, the whaling industry is better viewed as a huge quantity of capital attempting to earn the highest pos-sible return. If it can exterminate whales in ten years and make 15 percent profit, but it could only make 10 percent with a sustainable harvest, then it will exterminate them in ten years. After that, the money will be moved to exterminating some other resource." It is very important for biologists to remember this view of the world because it seems to be strongly carried over into the area of biological resource planning.

Let us now take a brief look at the way ecosystem services are delivered. If we look at the complexity of natural ecosystems, we can, to a degree, identify in them some critical control points. These control points regulate the flows of energy and nutrients in the ecosystem; two are absolutely cru-cial. The first is that obscure group of immobile organisms called plants. With a few trivial exceptions, ecosystems do not work without producers that can capture energy directly from the sun—the green plants. Get rid of the producer trophic level, and at a stroke the ecosystem itself is destroyed.

The second crucial control point is at the other end of the cycle. Plants take up nutrients with the help of fungi and bacteria. But what would hap-pen after they had taken up all the available nutrients in the system if there were no decomposers? The whole system would grind to a halt unless there were some way of freeing up those nutrients for the next generation. That is where the decomposers, large and small, come into the picture.

Theoretically, an ecosystem that had nothing in it but producers and decomposers could exist. These decomposers include bacteria and fungi, of which zoos do not have exhibits. But zoos do have exhibits of some of the many different kinds of animals that do crucial jobs in decomposing. These range from vultures that devour carcasses and dung beetles that take care of animal waste down to much smaller creatures. There are possibly as many species of mites as there are species of insects, a vast number. Many of them are decomposers that live in the soil. They are very poorly known, but if we took a handful of rich soil, put it in a funnel, put a light over the funnel and a bottle of alcohol underneath it, we would get a great variety of animals dropping out. There may be hundreds of species of mites, tiny worms, little insects, and other creatures. These organisms help with the absolutely crucial job of taking apart those very complex organic molecules that have been built by plants and larger animals, and breaking them down through a complex series of processes into the kinds of nutrients that can be taken up again by the plants to keep the whole process going.

To repeat, when the ecosystem is disrupted at either the producer or decomposer level, all the ecosystem's services end because the ecosystem does not exist anymore. Every time we remove a plant species, we probably eliminate something on the order of ten animal species. A cascading series of losses occurs, so one always has to pay very careful attention to plants.

Between the plants and the decomposers are a varied array of consumers: the herbivores eat the plants directly, the first level of predators eats the herbivores, another level of predators eats the first level of predators, and so on. From all the levels of the food chain right to the top predators, a flow of energy is being fed into the decomposer level, both in the form of bodies and in the form of wastes. There are also very complex relationships at the consumer level, which are needed to keep the rest of the game going. Such relationships include the roles played by pollinators of many plants.

If one looks carefully at the major control points of an ecosystem, one usually finds that many species are involved. Both major controllers and minor controllers usually can be identified. Systems may vary, however, in their degree of complexity. For example, a redwood forest is less diverse than a tropical forest and control is clearly vested largely in a single species of tree. The redwoods fix most of the solar energy; take up and retain most of the nutrients; exercise important control over water, air flow, and the microclimate in the forest; filter out pollution; and provide other services. This one species has an enormous amount of control over both structure and flow, even though other controllers may be present. Yet the critical factor in the redwood forest may actually be mycorrhizal fungi that permit the redwoods to exist. Conversely, in a tropical rainforest a wide variety of controllers may occur in a single area: hundreds of varieties of trees in a couple of hectares rather than the same species of tree covering many hectares. Thus, one could find a single species of tree being the major controller in an ecosystem, or one could find a single species of tree being just a minor controller but a member of the controlling guild. But, as I indicated with the example of the mycorrhizal fungi, ecosystems are not simple, and it is difficult to figure out what really controls what.

One particularly good example of how difficult it is to judge the role of an organism in an ecosystem comes to mind. I did some field work about 15 years ago in Australia, and I was looking for a moth called *Cactoblastis cactorium*. This is a moth that feeds on *Opuntia* cactus, an easily identified cactus now very scattered and relatively rare in Queensland. I found a few bunches of *Opuntia* but could not find on them any infestation of larvae of this tiny moth. If I had been just dumped into Queensland with no prior knowledge, I would have assumed that the cactuses were only a very minor element in the ecosystem. Historically, we know that this has not been the case. *Opuntia* was introduced into Australia from South America in 1840, and by the beginning of this century Queensland was overrun with the prickly pear cactus. Much of the state—some 75,000 square miles—became a solid growth of *Opuntia*, which virtually destroyed the cattle industry in large areas. *Opuntia* became the dominant feature of the ecosystem of much of Queensland and part of New South Wales. Entomologists then found in South America a little moth that fed on the cactus. The moth was imported into Australia and it devoured the *Opuntia*. Today the *Opuntia* exists as a fugitive species in rare clumps: eventually, a single *Cactoblastis* female moth will find a clump, lay its eggs, build a population on the clump, destroy the clump, and disperse. Perhaps one of those females that disperses will find another clump. The cactus is rare, and one could claim that the dominant controller in the ecosystems of Queensland is actually this hard-to-find moth that keeps the *Opuntia* cactus from taking over.

So there are great difficulties in trying to figure out what is important in an ecosystem, what species have major control, and what the impact will be of deleting A, B, or C. If somebody offered us a billion dollars to let him press a button and make the *Cactoblastis* moth disappear from Queensland, we could easily get the Queensland government to pay us two billion dollars not to do it because, even though one can scarcely find that little moth today, it is essential.

Some broad conclusions can be made about the impacts of extinctions on ecosystem functions. First of all, there is obviously a quantitative consideration. It would be much more catastrophic, all else being equal, to eliminate an entire group or guild of organisms that does essentially the same thing than to eliminate a single species—for example, to take out all the trees rather than one species of tree from a mixed forest. Experiments have not been done to demonstrate this, for both ethical and logistical reasons. But "experiments" have been done often enough in the past for us to know that when a huge area of forest is clear-cut, it is often very difficult for the forest ecosystem to regenerate, particularly if it is a tropical forest. Conversely, a tropical moist forest ecosystem may not be destroyed even though loggers have gone in and dragged out every teak tree in the whole area.

A second point can be mentioned about impacts on ecosystem functioning: eliminating a "K-selected" species is likely to have a worse effect on ecosystem functions than deleting an "r-selected" species. A K-selected species is one that tends to reproduce itself very slowly, produce very few offspring, and give each offspring a very good chance of survival. Elephants and human beings are K-selected. Cockroaches, houseflies, and some kinds of fishes are r-selected—they produce huge numbers of offspring and often can build large populations extremely rapidly. If elephants are exterminated in an area, they cannot be restored in two years of elephant breeding; if houseflies are wiped out, we can be up to our necks in houseflies again in two years. One could say that the only K-selected species we could reduce to very small numbers and as a general result help all the ecosystems on the planet is, very clearly, *Homo sapiens*.

In summary, the worst impacts will occur following extinctions of producers or decomposers, when entire guilds are deleted as opposed to particular species, and when K-selected species rather than r-selected species are removed.

Now what kinds of impacts will there be? They can range from negligible to catastrophic. When the elms disappeared from the eastern forests in North America, there apparently were not any serious problems, although it may be that studies of the disappearance were not done properly. At any rate, no problems were noticed immediately. However, some ecosystem disruptions have gained everyone's attention and produced "disruption syndromes" that have become quite famous. The best known one at the moment is probably desertification, which is going on at a disastrous rate all over the world. Such disruptions remove a whole series of ecosystem services, including the important "climate-ameliorating service" of plants. If trees and other vegetation are cleared from an area, not only is valuable food and forage for animals destroyed but the climate often is changed in such a way that it is impossible for the original vegetation to return.

Deforestation in the tropics produces extraordinarily severe results because of the poor soils that frequently underlie tropical forests and because so much of the nutrient material is contained in the plants themselves. When a tropical forest is removed, regeneration of any kind is extremely difficult. Ecological services, such as the climate-amelorating service, are lost along with the forest.

One of the most frightening problems we are rapidly learning more about is the problem of the earth's toxification. The most prominent manifestation of this, at the moment, is acid rain (although there are many others such as the effects of PCBs). A colleague of mine in China measured rain in 1981 with a pH roughly that of lemon juice. It turns out that dousing entire ecosystems with dilute acid is not the way to encourage them to continue delivering their services.

Recently, *New Scientist* magazine quoted a German biochemist (August 12, 1982) who predicted that forests in parts of Europe have been irreversibly damaged. Changes that acid rain have already caused in the soil are possibly irreversible, and in the next decade a progressive die-off of most of the forests of central Europe may occur. If that is true, it may mean that many of the other forests of the Northern Hemisphere are also on their way out. It is possible that rain-induced acidification of the soil can change the soil biota so that the biota itself starts acidifying. A positive-feedback downhill spiral is created. Nitrogen-fixing enzymes do not do too well when the pH gets below three, and bacteria are not good at buffering themselves against outside environmental changes. It is quite conceivable that if society continues dumping into the atmosphere large quantities of nitrogen oxides and sulfur oxides, which are the principal sources of acid rain, the life-support machinery of the planet could be damaged to the extent that humanity will be lucky to survive as small hunter and gatherer groups in less-polluted areas of the Southern Hemisphere.

Another syndrome that other speakers have discussed is the problem of "weedification." Many organisms—from English sparrows and mongooses to Kudzu vines and *Optunia*—are carried from place to place by humanity but have become enormous agents of extinction in their new environments. Anyone who has gone to Hawaii to see some of the native drepanidid finches knows what I mean. Indian mynah birds and American cardinals are everywhere, but most native species, including species especially adapted to pollinating the native plants, are extraordinarily difficult to find.

By causing extinctions, humanity can have enormous impacts on ecosystems, impacts that tend to destroy the very services we depend on those systems to provide. For example, if the trees of the Amazon Basin are chopped down, it is not at all unlikely that the climate may change so that wheat cannot be grown in our own Middle West. Because the Middle West of North America is by far the leading food exporting area of the entire world, that would not be a trivial consequence.

How easily can ecosystem services be restored once severe damage has been done? Krakatoa has been used as an example to suggest that it is relatively easy. Many people remember Krakatoa as the volcanic island west of Java that exploded, was recolonized, and regrew a fine tropical forest. It is, in fact, a classic example in the island biogeography of birds because returning bird species showed the kind of pattern of reestablishment and equilibrium that was predicted by Robert MacArthur and Ed Wilson (1967) in their classic work on island biogeography. Unfortunately, the rest of the world is not Krakatoa. When an ecosystem is destroyed, it does not usually have rich natural systems surrounding it from which propagules can come to repopulate it. The areas humanity destroys are not small islands that have their climate controlled by the surrounding sea or that have a nice rich layer of volcanic ash for the reestablishment of plants. Generally, the scenario is more likely to unfold as it has in portions of eastern Brazil and Costa Rica, where forests have been cleared for grazing cattle. The ranchers found that cattle could not be grazed after seven or eight years, and now only a wasteland remains.

It turns out that if there is to be a natural process of succession that restores the original ecosystem there must be both the proper substrate and a source of propagules—that is, organisms that can repopulate. As Aldo Leopold said years ago, the first rule of intelligent tinkering is to save all the cogs and wheels. We have not been saving the cogs and wheels that are necessary to reestablish ecosystems.

This raises the question of substituting things that were not in the original system. Hal Mooney and I searched the literature with a lot of help from our friends, and it turns out that it is not all that easy to find successful substitutions of one organism for another. First of all, it is very difficult to predict how a controller or a noncontroller in one system will perform in another. Organisms that were minor controllers in an original ecosystem may turn out to be major controllers in a new one. All we have to do is remember the Kudzu vine or the mongoose or the goats that have been introduced onto islands to know what havoc can be wrought by the wrong introduction, even when the organism seemed to be quite innocuous in its original ecosystem where predators and parasites had coevolved.

A second important point that was brought out very well in Dr. Morton's earlier discussion is that organisms tend to be extraordinarily fine-tuned to the environments in which they live. A classic example is the failure of the British to reestablish the large copper butterfly, which had become extinct in its original habitat, by introducing very similar Dutch stocks to England. Despite the controlled circumstances, it simply has not worked, and the reason is that the Dutch stock is just a slightly different ecotype with very subtly different ecological requirements. It cannot make a go of it, even in a very similar habitat.

We are finding the same thing in some of the reintroduction experiments we have made with butterflies in North America. Foresters know very well that if they try to plant, say, Douglas firs in a new area, the stock of seeds for replanting has to come from an area very similar in altitude, latitude, and longitude. From our works with butterflies, I think this sort of close fine-tuning to the environment will prove true of most herbivorous insects, and it probably goes much further than that. The problem is not merely one of restocking with the same species, it is one of getting the same genetic stock, or basically, the same ecotype. We are not sure exactly how close it has to be, but apparently it must be closer than most people have assumed.

I agree wholeheartedly with the comments presented at this symposium about the chances of successful reintroductions from zoo stock. I think zoos play an extraordinarily important role in the world, and there can be no objection whatsoever to their attempting to maintain, in perpetuity, organisms that are declining in the wild or that have become extinct. These are efforts to save something precious. However, I think that only in rare cases and at extraordinary cost will it be possible to maintain organisms for very long in zoos and then successfully reintroduce them into any natural habitat that just happens to be left. There will be exceptions. It is possible that Dr. Thomas Cade's work in conserving and reintroducing peregrine falcons to the eastern United States will turn out eventually to be a big success, and I hope it will be (Cade 1969; Cade et al. 1971). But in this case, the environmental change that caused extinctions, overuse of DDT, has been reversed. When we examine the costs and realize that there are something like 4,000 species of mammals alone that might have to be reintroduced, then the logistic impossibility of this approach becomes clear. It is false to think that, as long as there are zoos, we do not have to worry about biological diversity.

Returning to the issue of substitutions, I am not going to present a long list of failed experiments. But I will point out that in almost every case we found that species-for-species substitutions have been unsuccessful. Either the system deteriorates within a generation or so of the substitution, or, if the system is not degenerating, humanity has to continually inject energy into it to keep it going. This applies, for instance, to a lot of exotic tree plantations that have been established in various parts of the world. The soil flora and fauna have deteriorated steadily in these plantations, reducing nutrient cycling in the system and portending eventual collapse.

Wheat and corn have done a lousy job of substituting for prairie grasses in nutrient cycling and preserving soils. We have had almost no luck in substituting fish stocks. When the California sardine was wiped out, nothing moved in to take its place. As Norman Myers can tell you much better than I, when domestic cattle are moved into a semiarid African ecosystem they become a ghastly substitute for the local antelopes. Not only can the antelopes produce more meat because of their greater ability to take advantage of plants in the area but they also do not have to trek to water every day as cattle do. In making this trek, cattle trample the plants and soil and create larger and larger areas of desolation. That is one of the reasons why the Sahel famine was so catastrophic. Cattle are poor substitutes for the antelopes.

Things get even worse when you move into inorganic substitutes for ecosystem services. Herbert Bormann (1976) has written about the problems that arise when society cuts down a forest and attempts to substitute for it with artifacts. We have to build dams to prevent floods, whereas the forests formerly metered the water for us. Because dams silt up, particularly when the forest is gone, they are not permanent substitutions. We have to use plastics to replace timber the forest would have yielded on a sustained basis. There is more silt in the water, so we have to put money into more water purification plants. We have to have more smog control because the forest is no longer doing an automatic air-filtering service for us. We have lost the weather-ameliorating service of the forest, so we need more air conditioning. We have to create more recreational facilities, and so on.

All this takes energy. It takes capital. The story is the same for most inorganic substitutions. They all tend to require more fossil fuels, and the very process of getting and burning more fossil fuels puts additional stress on the natural systems. We get into another of these positive feedback systems that leads us into a downhill spiral.

Above all else, is the importance of preserving the genetic library. This is absolutely essential if humanity is to stay in the race to increase crop yields because agriculture depends in part on close relatives of crops for germ plasm (new or different genetic material). Genetic engineers cannot create new genes. They work with the genetic material that already exists. Every time we wipe out a genetically distinct population, whether it is the dusky seaside sparrow or a subspecies of chimpanzee, we are losing raw materials of potentially great benefit to humanity. There is no way to substitute for them. Those who think that molecular biologists will soon be building species to order ought to talk to a molecular biologist. He will laugh them out of his office. Even if they could build species to order, ecologists do not know enough about ecosystems and their functioning to know what to order. We could not possibly design species to fill an array of emptied niches.

There you have it. That is basically the story, but let me make a final comment. The problems we face are very clear. The answers to these problems do not lie strictly in the areas of conservation biology or population biology. We obviously must find strategies and tactics immediately to stop the development of wild lands. This will be impossible in many tropical areas, but that does not mean we should not search as hard as possible for ways of stopping it where it can be stopped. Nobody knows whether preserving 5, 10, 20, or 40 percent of the ecosystems in a relatively natural condition is necessary for the long-term persistence of society.

What we must remember is that when economists say, "It has always been like this," they mean back to the beginning of the Industrial Revolution. It seems that few economists have heard of anything before the Industrial Revolution. Most think the modern world—which they define as a world of perpetual growth, with continually more goods, services, and people—will fly apart without this growth. This has been called "the creed of the cancer cell." Ecologists tend to warn us against uncontrolled growth and emphasize that we really should not experiment to see how much we can destroy before the whole system collapses on us.

In my view, in a country like the United States there is not the slightest excuse for developing one more square inch of undisturbed land. If more housing for people is needed in the United States, then we should redevelop some blighted urban areas that could provide decent shelter if they were properly restored. The United States is very, very short of undisturbed land. The kinds of preservation efforts that Robert Jenkins discussed in his presentation illustrate the problems we face. We all know that these are strictly stopgap measures. The hallmark of our society must be changed from one of endless "development" to one of a sustainable, stable, self-renewing cycle of life. As much land must be preserved in a "virgin" state as possible. I put this in quotes because there is not a square inch of virgin land, land that has not been influenced by human activities, left on the planet. Every place is polluted with chlorinated hydrocarbons, has a changed set of radioisotopes, and so on because of human activities.

The second thing we must do is to make the areas that human beings already occupy much more habitable to other organisms. In places like Africa and Asia, ways must be found for people to make coexistence with elephants actually possible over the long-term. Closer to home, cementing over every stream in the United States that runs through a town must be stopped. The government should put money into tearing down some run-down motels and shopping centers and planting trees. And, more crucially, the flux of toxic substances into the atmosphere and into the oceans must be ended. After all, even if all the remaining "virgin" land is saved, if the acid rains continue, it is not going to make any difference. Above all, we are going to have to move toward a so-called "sustainable society" and negative population growth. The human population must gradually be reduced to a size that can be sustained in the long-term with everybody living a decent life. All this is very idealistic, I know, but in fact I think it is not really idealistic—it is the only practical way to go.

There are, however, some bright signs. The environment has become a standard issue everywhere in a relatively short time. The rate of population growth has slowed down in various areas, and the Chinese have shown that this can occur quite rapidly if there is the will. In principle, the values that we have been talking about in this symposium can be integrated into a realistic economic strategy (Krutilla and Fisher 1975). What needs to be done in the United States is for everyone to work very hard to control and reverse the environmental damage that has been done already. Basically, I think the stage is set for conservation to win. Whether the play will be completed before the theater burns down, however, remains to be seen.

References Cited and Additional Readings

Bormann, F. H.
   1976.   An inseparable linkage: conservation of natural ecosystems and the conservation of fossil energy, *Bioscience* 26:754–60.

Brown, L. R.
   1980.   *Food or Fuel: New Competition for the World's Cropland.* Washington, D.C.: Worldwatch Institute.

Cade, T. J., J. L. Lincer, C. M. White, D. G. Roseneau, and L. G. Swartz.
1971.   DDT residues and eggshell changes in Alaskan falcons and hawks. *Science* 172:955−57.

Cade, T. J.
1969.   The northern peregrine populations. In *Peregrine Falcon Populations: Their Biology and Decline*, ed. J. J. Hickey. Madison: The University of Wisconsin Press, 502−5.

Ehrenfeld, D.
1978.   *The Arrogance of Humanism*. New York: Oxford University Press.

Ehrlich, P. R. and H. A. Mooney.
1983.   Extinction, substitution, and ecosystem services. *Bioscience* 33: 248−54.

Krutilla, J. V. and A. C. Fisher.
1975.   *The Economics of Natural Environments*. Baltimore: Johns Hopkins University Press.

MacArthur, R. H. and E. O. Wilson.
1967.   *The Theory of Island Biogeography*. Princeton: Princeton University Press.

Pearce, F.
1982.   The menace of acid rain. *The New Scientist*, August 12, 1982, 419.

Simon, J.
1980.   Resources, population, environment: an oversupply of false bad news. *Science* 208:1431−35.

12

Cultural Loss Can Foreshadow Human Extinctions: The Influence Of Modern Civilization

COLIN M. TURNBULL

In addressing the final topic in this symposium, I want to try and provoke in you some of the thoughts that the topic has provoked in me—from the point of view of a social and cultural anthropologist. Because of the cultures that I have worked with, particularly in Africa, I have increasingly felt an enormous loss in my own life at the growing distance between our human culture and the wider natural world of which I have come to believe we humans are an integral part. I might have learned sooner about this integrity, this wholeness of the natural world, had my early education included the wisdom to which you have been exposed at this symposium. As it is, I learned it from the Mbuti people of Africa, who firmly believe that they cannot possibly survive if the natural world around them, or any one part of that world, ceases to survive.

It is important to include the realm of humans in our symposium because we, too, are animals and because one of our human specialties is the business of extinction. As animals, we are subject to the same natural forces that can and do lead to the physical extinction of other life forms. But no animal except ourselves is capable of bringing extinction to all life forms, including its own, as we are now capable of doing.

We humans are a special case in a number of respects, two of which particularly interest me. The first is our enormous range of adaptability, a range shared with some of the animals already discussed here, but which goes beyond them. We all know that humans can live in a wide range of environments, from sea level up to habitations of well over 10,000 feet, 2 miles up in the air. We can live in the polar regions, in the equatorial forests, in arid deserts, and in extremely moist climates. We are enormously adaptable, and this gives us something rather dangerous: a confidence in our ability to survive under almost any conditions. The second pertinent factor is the intellectual power of *Homo sapiens* for abstract thought: we can conceive of problems before they arise. We can, when we are willing to do so, consider possible solutions without dangerously resorting to trial and error. Thanks to this intellectual power, we have vastly increased the habitable areas of the world. It is now technologically possible for a human being to be born, live, and to die not just on the surface of the earth but underground, up in the air, on the sea, under the sea, and, potentially, out in space. This power has also made us far too confident of our chances of survival and of our ability to overcome difficulties that arise along the way. This confidence in our physical survival blinds us to the possibility of another form of extinction we face, which we will call here "cultural extinction."

Cultural extinction has already been discussed in this symposium with regard to other animals. Culture, as anthropologists define it, is learned behavior and traditions that by and large are adaptive and work toward survival. So in this sense, animals have culture, too. Animals may undergo abrupt or gradual cultural extinction in various ways. This process is, in fact, the first step toward their physical extinction. Ironically, it can come about through our own well-intentioned efforts to preserve or conserve other animals. For example, the moment a game reserve is established, the environment is changed just by that fact of human intervention. Life within the habitat, its social organization and behavior and even its physiological form, very slowly begins to change. The process becomes more dramatic the moment we fence the reserve in, particularly if we introduce tourists, as often happens to raise money necessary for the upkeep of the reserve. When we establish a zoo—when we put animals in cages—we are causing the most extreme form of environmental change and even more dramatic changes in animal behavior may occur. In addition to the loss of certain physiological abilities, even the ability to reproduce may be lost. But I will certainly agree with earlier speakers who believe that, by all means, it is often important that we intervene in these ways despite uncertainties. Just the fact that we do not know precisely why we should *not* intervene is reason enough to do so rather than to allow life forms to die out merely because we did not know all the answers.

Domestication is another form of human intervention that can cause cultural change and, possibly, extinction amongst animals. What, for example, has happened to the dog and the cat? What relationship is there, other than a distant hereditary link, between the tiny, coiffeured "toy" poodle confined in an apartment and its ancestor the wolf? I am not saying that domestication is wrong. I am merely just recognizing that under conditions of domestication, life forms may change almost beyond recognition. For the dog and the cat, domestication was, among other things, a change from an original system of interdependency upon many other life forms to an artificially induced system of dependency upon one particular life form, ourselves. The pet cat or dog in the city could hardly survive without our care or at the least without the edible refuse that we discard with such abandon. They have become parasites. We must keep this process in mind when we begin to examine the insidious changes that can take place in our own human lives. Modern civilization—comparable to the game reserve or even to the zoo in changing our environment—may very well prove to be a cage we have built for ourselves, a cage necessitating changes in our own social behavior. These changes have, I am afraid, set us upon a road to dehumanization. They are radically changing our culture, and, if the process continues, shall make us as different from what we once were as the wild cats and dogs are from their domestic counterparts. We, too, have become overly dependent, not upon other animals, but upon our own mechanical creations. I am not advocating the elimination of technology. Modern technology is a major and positive feature of our civilization that helps us to survive physically. But it may be slowly extinguishing us culturally. We have become dependent on machines, yet we do not even like to think about this dependency, let alone admit it. What would happen if we removed one single human artifact, say the electric generator, from existence right at this moment? All the lights in this auditorium would go out. Who here has brought a flashlight? We might file out in an orderly manner, but it would be perfectly possible that confusion could lead to disorder that could lead to panic and chaos. Once out onto the street, the loss of public transportation would force us to bicycle or walk home. At home the food in our refrigerators would spoil within a few days. In any case, how would we cook it? Where would we find wood in urban areas or matches if the factories that make matches go out of operation because of the same defunct generators? This one artifact alone reaches into many truly vital aspects of our lives.

This scenario is perhaps unthinkable, and all I am trying to illustrate is the fact that we have become far more dependent on modern technology than we may realize, and that, if excessive, this dependency could be disastrous. Much more than mere inconvenience or a change in our standard of living, however, is at stake. We could adjust to the loss of some of our modern technology because of our adaptability. But the pervasiveness of modern technology has begun an insidious process. As a result, we are at risk of losing our very essence, our very identity, our humanity itself.

To begin with, how do we define our humanity? At the very least, what most of us consider to be the essence of our humanity is our ability to interact with each other in a "civilized" or at least a "social" manner. However, in my experience civilized behavior in this sense is rather more often found amongst "primitives" than it is amongst "civilized" societies. Primitive societies are based on reciprocity, on rules of reciprocal behavior rooted in mutual needs. In such a context, it is not a question of getting what I want from you by buying it. I can only get what I want from you, in a truly social system, by returning to you something that you yourself need. What is at stake is mutual need and satisfaction—not exact equivalence. That is the essence of social reciprocity. It reaches its highest form in values that not one of us in this room, I am sure, would deny: consideration, compassion, caring, kindness, and that remarkable human phenomenon we call love.

There are different forms of love, and love can be something, no matter what some people will argue, that human populations can lose. And with that loss, they lose their humanity. I worked amongst such a people, the Ik, in northern Uganda. These people are a convincing example that this loss of the capacity to love can happen to human population under at least one set of circumstances. Ironically, for the Ik this process began with the creation of the Kidepo Game Reserve in northern Uganda. To preserve game in this reserve, it was suggested that the people who were hunters and gatherers there move from the enclosed valley and become farmers. One population did so and became very successful crop farmers. Others, unfortunately, retreated up into the surrounding barren mountains where there was no livelihood possible of the kind they had once known and where conditions steadily worsened as the Sahelian desiccation, a drying up of the land, spread. Thus began, a mere three-generations ago, the process of cultural change and extinction of the Ik. Up in those barren mountains the Ik needed food, but there was nothing to hunt. They were not allowed down into the park. Even worse, their traditional migration patterns were eliminated by the establishment of enforced political boundaries that could no longer be traversed in search of game.

The Ik at first tried farming, but with four inches of rainfall a year and very bad soil, these resources proved to be pitifully inadequate. They decided, quite correctly, that farming was not worth the energy expended. They became scavengers. But the few water holes they had—only two for about nine villages where I was—were polluted. It would be suicidal to drink from them. To get a drink, a person had to look for butterflies on the surface of the sandy soil, which generally indicated some subsurface moisture. He or she would dig down and find maybe half a cupful of water — enough to keep one person alive for half-a-day or so while searching for food. In two years with these people, I very seldom came across enough food in any one spot, in the form of edible berries or roots, to satisfy more than one person. This meant that if one wished to survive physically amongst the Ik, the essential quest for food and water had to be conducted individually. It was just a hard, economic fact.

It does not matter for our immediate purposes whether this situation was induced by natural forces or by human intervention. What matters is simply the condition of change; the terrible resultant total breakdown of the family and social relationships. Caring for others and taking social responsibility had become mutually reciprocal values and actions that were simply unworkable. They had become dysfunctional in Ik society. No Ik who wished to survive could afford to care whether anyone else survived, even a husband or a wife. There was simply no predictable, practical way for one person to help another. I have seen an individual go off for the day's food and come back three weeks later. Those luckier might possibly come back three hours later. It was completely unpredictable. So even if a husband and wife were to start scavenging at the same time, neither might come back the same day. For a period of one year, I saw spouses constantly coming and going from a house and not once did I see both spouses there together. Under such conditions, pregnancies become ghastly accidents because an Ik woman recognizes what a threat to her own survival a pregnancy would be. However, it was economically expedient, sometimes, for a young woman to risk getting pregnant when cattle herders, forced by drought, came up into the foothills, leaving their women behind. Young Ik girls could get milk and blood from the strangers' cattle, adding to their immediate chances of survival. But in return they could get pregnant. This made them angry, then bored, and that is not a very good beginning for the life of any child.

An Ik mother, quite remarkably, does not destroy her child, although she gives it every chance to destroy itself. She will feed it for three years. At the end of two years, she begins to abuse the child by beating it, letting it crawl into fires, and laughing at it. This seemed inhuman to me at the time. I wrote back a report saying this was as barbaric and savage a behavior as I had ever seen in Africa—that the Ik were inhuman. I was wrong. The Ik were not at all inhuman. On the contrary, their behavior was very,

very human. And it was a lot more social than one might imagine because, in a sense, a mother was caring about her child when she did these things. She was teaching her child the essential lesson of physical survival in that particular environment: "In a year from now, you will be on your own, baby." This ştarts, remember, in the child's second year; in the third year— out. But by throwing the children out at three years old, the Ik are again giving them their best chance at survival. And when the mother laughed at the child, she was giving it another important educational lesson in the game of physical survival: "When you fall into a ravine and twist your an- kle, the chances are I will be ten miles away, so I won't be there to pull you out; and even if I were there, I would just sit back and laugh because there would not be anything I could do anyway." The ravines are perhaps 70 degrees in slope, dropping as much as 500 feet. The Ik are always on the verge of starvation; they can barely raise enough energy to scavenge. Tem- peratures rise to more than 100 degrees. So the mother is right. She is teaching the child an essential lesson. It is a form of caring, but few of us would recognize it as such.

Typically, the children form gangs and live together for a few brief years—but they do not help each other. They are highly competitive, and even within a gang the first child to get to any food gets it all. The food may be bits of figs left over after baboons have eaten. When the kids are old enough to climb trees and compete with the baboons for whole figs, they move up into the senior gang. Each new arrival is the smallest, and so is the least likely to get food and the most likely to die. It is the same old story—the fittest survive very, very nicely. When the Ik reach adulthood, at about age 13, they have learned the lesson that survival is an individual game. They have learned how to survive physically but at an enormous cultural cost. Their stockaded villages are isolated, almost hostile, and not an integral part of the environment (Figure 1). Inside, each compound is tightly walled against the neighboring compounds. The villages are di- vided into sections, each with its own house, isolated, looking outwards from the center. Every individual compound has its own separate entrance or exit, and there is no communal village center.

The Ik have a word for "good"—*marang*, and a saying for "a good man"—*iakw anamarang*. One might think *iakw anamarang* would be someone who gave food to another. Not a bit. A man who gives away food would be a foolish man. This expression means "a man who has food in his stomach," and it must be in his actual stomach—not in any stupid granary where someone can steal it.

I met one girl of about 11 or 12 years who was the last girl that had been

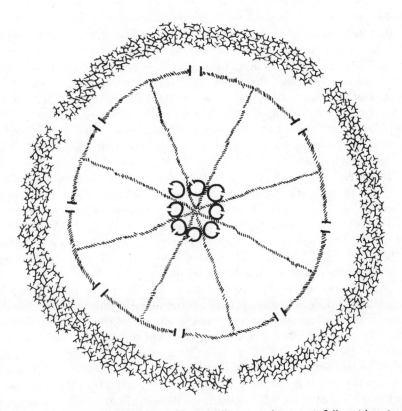

Figure 1   *Village structure of Ik in Uganda. Ik unsociality is painfully evident in the ground plan of their villages. Each individual compound is isolated from all others by a thick, impenetrable eight-foot stockade and has its own, often booby-trapped, entrance. There is no meeting place inside any village, for there is no socialization. Each individual's compound is forbidden to all others and is an empty space facing outwards. The only cooperation required is in the casual maintenance of the rough thorn fence around the perimeter of the village for protection against predators such as leopards and lions. The inner stockades, made of heavy wood, are individually built in a much more business-like manner, for they are to protect neighbor from neighbor. The emphasis on individual survival and self-interest goes far beyond the mere physical structure of the village, however. It has come to permeate every aspect of human relationships among the Ik. Illustration by Sally Bensusen.*

truly cared for by her family. She had been cared for when a "family" was still economically feasible in an effective sense. Adupa's parents were able to feed her a little beyond three years, and she never learned the necessary lesson of independence. She continued to be dependent upon her parents until finally, as the Sahelian desiccation process engulfed the Ik, her parents could not even feed themselves and had to leave her to get food on her own. But she had not learned even that. Unable to feed her, her parents walled her up in a compound right next to the compound I was in. Ten days later, they came back and threw the body out. That was the end of Adupa, and everyone laughed and said, "You see, that is what happens if you love each other."

There is a kind of dignity in Ik behavior—they will refuse food when they are going to die because eating would be a waste. I saw this happen many times. They prefer food to be given to someone who they feel needs it. For them, this is neither the children nor the aged but the breeding group. With a healthy breeding group, the Ik may perhaps survive as a population. That is sound biology. It is also a form of caring, even though it isn't precisely what we would call humanity.

In Ik society, caring can be dysfunctional. There was an Ik man who was killed by love. He was old enough to remember days when people did care for each other. Although he had dysentery and needed care, his wife, who also was very foolish and loved him, had to leave him and go off in search of food for herself to survive. The woman had been away for about three days when this fellow decided that his house was so foul because of the dysentery that he would go down the mountainside to get some grass and make a thatch shelter so that his wife would have a nice clean place when she came back. I had given him some medicine that made him a little stronger, but he was not strong enough. He went down, gathered the grass, and was trying to carry it back up the mountainside when he apparently laid down to sleep. That was where I found him and took his photograph. But he was not asleep, he was dead.

While I was with the Ik, there was a Turkana raid. In the process, someone was killed and everyone fled to build another village. An old man was lying on the ground flat on his stomach and moving very slowly in the direction that everyone else was moving. A youth stepped over the man, and I said, "Who is that?" I had not seen him before, and I wanted to put his name down in my kinship charts. And the youth replied—this is literally what he said—"Oh, that's no one, that's my father." So I noted that and asked, "Why don't you carry him? He needs some help." When he asked me why he should carry him I said, "Because I will give you some food." I was bribing a starving person; the youth himself was close to death. So he picked his old father up and carried him on his back, getting him to the foot of the first hill. But then everyone started laughing at him, so he dumped the old man on the ground and said to me that he did not want my food; I could carry the old man myself. He was absolutely right; there was really no justifiable point to the whole exercise. All that I was doing was satisfying my own feelings of right and wrong and interfering in a natural process without thinking out all the consequences. But I carried the father to safety and tried to nurse him back to health. When I left the Ik, not much later, I left that old man enough food, and enough money with the border police, to have kept him alive in comfort for a full year. I learned later that within two weeks he was dead. I knew perfectly well it was going to happen. If I was going to give assistance, I should have tried to give it to the breeding group for, as the Ik say, at least they can have more children.

When Lolim, the last ritual priest still alive, went off to die, he walked to a ridge from which he could face the sacred mountain, Morungole, where Ik religious beliefs hold that God set man down on earth. Lolim, still believing that maybe there was more to goodness than having food in your stomach, had been one who shared food and had thus attracted ridicule. His own son had refused to let him die in his house. A short time later, his widow was moving along with the village. She was blind, and on the way she fell down into a ravine. The Ik, who were in a good mood that day, came to my compound and said, "Hey, you have got to come see this, it is the funniest thing ever." The old woman was lying on her back in the ravine, waving her arms and legs in the air, and everyone was shouting, "*Ka'e, Ka'e,* turtle, turtle." Once again, I tried to intervene, feeling that I was helping her by focusing on her individual physical survival. A colleague who was with me also came and treated her wounds. We gave her food and told her to come and stay with us. She refused, saying that she wanted to die near her son. And we said, "But your son would not let your husband die near him; he certainly is not going to let you." And she replied, "I know, but at least I'd like to be as near as I can." Then occurred one of the most horrible things that has ever happened to me in the field: this old lady started to cry. Tears started out of her blind eyes, and the most awful sounds from her mouth, and she said that she was crying because we had reminded her of the days when people cared for each other. And she would rather not have remembered that people used to care for each other; it hurt too much. If that is not cultural extinction, I do not know what is.

So I suggest that relationships and behaviors thought to be integral to human society and culture *can* be lost. The Ik family structure has simply died—the family is no longer functional. Reciprocal relationships, the foundation of many societies, are equally dysfunctional. Survival lies in each individual's hands. It is wrong to think that this could never happen to us and therefore has nothing to do with us. Look at our own lives. We can be a good deal like the Ik. When I came back to New York City after living for two years with the Ik, my immediate reaction was, "Ha! Now I understand how this place works." In this environment, which modern civilization has created for us, with its specific problems of human density and diversity, about the only way we can survive is to ignore 99 percent of the human beings around us. Otherwise, we would go beserk overnight. Economically, there is no way we could care effectively for all we see who are in need. We may give a beggar some pocket money and hope never to see him again. But who amongst us has really ever cared for one beggar *fully*, taking him off the street, giving him shelter, food, work, an education, or whatever else he needs; in other words, taken *full* responsibility for him as another human being? Very few of us can afford to do this, so we have to shut each other out of our lives. That is just one of the byproducts of western civilization, one of the ways it has affected our horizons of sociability.

When I was a child (I came from a British background that was comfortable but neither excessively rich nor poor) I was compelled to "help" as soon as I was able. I remember well a very early chore, helping my mother roll up knitting wool simply by holding out my hands. We had hours of conversation doing this, and it was a wonderful opportunity for communication. As soon as I was a little bit older, and more able, I was made to help my father with more physical jobs. I also was made to help the servants and therefore introduced to the whole British social network of beautifully stratified interdependency: the cook could order me to do things while the parlor maid could only *ask* me to do things—but I had to do them either way. My reward—certainly never cash—was the recognition that my individual survival depended upon my fulfilling obligations toward other human beings. These included not only our household but the distant families of aunts and uncles, as well as immediate neighbors. We children were sent all over the place to do chores in return for which we received not one cent, not one candy bar. We might receive thanks or a hug, but the real reward, and I remember realizing it quite consciously at that early age, was this grand recognition: Good Heavens! All these people owe me something! This is true social security, and it is also the way a social system works: through social reciprocity. I am not saying it is moral and altruistic; I did not believe that even at the time. It is merely the hard recognition of where your own survival lies.

When we look back at all the things the Industrial Revolution has done to us as well as for us, we tend to think that at least it took poverty away and made life "easier." Actually, it seems to have merely exported poverty to the Third World and shifted it around in our own world. Western civilization has made some of us wealthier at the expense of others, but it certainly has not made us equal. Has it improved the standard of living? Yes, to some extent. It has brought great benefits, but it also has done some very dangerous things. One of the major early consequences was the introduction and spread of the use of cash and the replacement of barter and trade by a cash economy. Until a person had access to cash, it was impossible for an individual to amass a considerable amount of wealth. Wealth—even in the form of land—was not readily transferable. An ordinary individual who was not a landowner was likely to be as rich or as poor as the next, but at least he or she had each other to rely on and exploit through a web based on kinship, territory, class, age, and other types of bonding considerations. Cash, however, made an enormous difference to our whole perception of survival. Individual survival suddenly became, or seemed to become, possible. We began to see our individual survival not in terms of a network of interpersonal obligations, beginning with the family, but in terms of our individual bank balances.

This kind of independence can be the death of sociality and the antithesis of humanity, which is the fundamental network of interpersonal relationships and of interdependencies that underly any "society." Although modern civilization is not necessarily the nemesis of humanity, it certainly puts the weapons in our hands to destroy ourselves and our families culturally. Having required too little of the growing child, the family will abruptly say to the young adult, "You are on your own now, we gave you a good education, go buy your own car or get whatever you need for yourself—a job (or, your own welfare payments)." And the father and mother may even consciously try to be as independent from one another as possible; each feeling it "right" to have their own independent income. We begin to shut each other off, and cash has made that possible. What seems to be happening is that we are beginning to put blinkers on our social horizons, our horizons of caring, and to narrow those horizons down bit by bit—just as the Ik have done, though for very different reasons.

Machines, as I said, have done other things to us: they have increasingly made us become physically dependent upon them and decreasingly dependent upon one another. Of course, human beings are needed to operate machines. But that is precisely what we have become—the tools of machines. We are just machine operators and do not feel we need each other except as such. We relate to each other as *categories*, with little if any sense of *human* responsibility. How many shoppers feel a sense of responsibility for the checkout clerk at the counter? The vast bulk of people we meet every day of our lives we relate to, if at all, as mere categories and not as fully reciprocating, caring, compassionate, concerned human beings. We are on our way down a path, a path not unlike the Ik's. I think I learned this most of all from another African people, the Mbuti, when I compared my own culture with theirs. The Mbuti culture is almost the polar opposite of that of the Ik.

I learned with the Mbuti that love is something much more than what so frequently replaces it in the developed world: mere self-gratification. I learned that love is a responsibility, and that it is a real and heavy (though welcome) burden to carry. And it is something that does not come easily; it is not our "natural" heritage nor a biological imperative. The Mbuti people work extremely hard in the forests as hunters. But they do not consider hunting and gathering their vegetables as "work." This activity is merely to fill their stomachs. For them, real "work" is loving your husband, loving your wife and child, loving your parents, and loving your friends. They work at it every moment of the day, and they actually call this "work." Indeed, many other traditional African societies besides the Mbuti refer to the maintenance of reciprocal relationships as "work." Some people have been pleased to call such societies "savage."

Linguistically, in the area where I worked and, I believe, in many other African languages, the words "need," "want," and "love" are all expressed by a single word. In this way, it is impossible for a man to love a woman without needing her. It is impossible for him to need her without wanting her. Now, to me, this attitude defines a human people, and a human culture, because the focus is totally on human relationships.

The Mbuti live in the Ituri forest in the nation of Zaire. This forest area is one of the few still relatively unaffected by Western civilization, and it may give us a clue as to what we might have once been like before we were touched by modern civilization. It is a natural world that still provides the Mbuti with everything they need. There is no such thing as polluted water in the forest. I have lived there on and off for seven years, and I have never once become sick in the forest. It is not surprising, then, that as the Mbuti walk through this forest they shout and sing to it. Of course this is also a good safety measure because it scares away predators that may be lurking around. But they are not shouting "Go away you nasty buffalo" or anything like that. They sing "father forest, mother forest"—*eba ndura, ema ndura*. And they are not just being romantic so that an anthropologist can go back and write an interesting, romantic book. They are very practical human beings who see themselves as a part of a total ecosystem. They see themselves as being *bamiki ba ndura*—"children of the forest." They say, "The forest gives us everything we need; it gives us our food, our shelter, our clothing." Then they add *a kondi su to*, which means "and also it loves us." This is dependency as it should be, as perceived by human beings interdependent with a natural world from which they have not removed themselves.

The Mbuti camps are almost indistinguishable from the forest itself, and their dwellings, made of saplings and leaves, are arranged roughly in circles. Each household in a camp faces inward toward a central, communal hearth (Figure 2). *Ndu* means "house," but linguistically *ndu* also means "womb." A house is a home in the sense of a womb. And the same root is part of the phrase, "father forest, mother forest (*ndura*)." These people are nothing if not consistent. They see this as an all-providing world. They do not try to disassociate themselves from other animals, and they recognize their equality in the forest.

Their concept of family is vastly different from ours. A Mbuti addresses and behaves toward any adult the age of his parents as mother or father. He can expect precisely the same treatment from them, and he has the same obligations toward them. The Mbuti definition of a family is "anyone who is living in the same territory at the same time because we are all dependent upon each other." This clearly expresses the value of *de*pendence as distinct from our value of *in*dependence.

Motherhood, also, is different conceptually. A woman becomes pregnant joyfully, and when she gives birth the whole camp celebrates. A couple of days before, she goes off and cuts a piece of fresh, sweet-smelling bark cloth to wrap the baby in and decorates it with the juice of the gardenia fruit. She puts a little bit of strong forest vine around the child's wrist, not in the superstitious belief that this vine will make the child strong, but as a symbol of her own faith in the forest and the knowledge—the absolute, certain knowledge—that her child, being a child of the forest, will grow tall and strong like that particular tree and have the qualities of the bark cloth and the gardenia, *eselé* and *kangé*. The newborn child is even washed with water found within a particular vine, a sweet-smelling, sacred water that is as close as you can get to the very essence of the forest, coming as it does from the heart of the forest itself. The lesson of this rec-

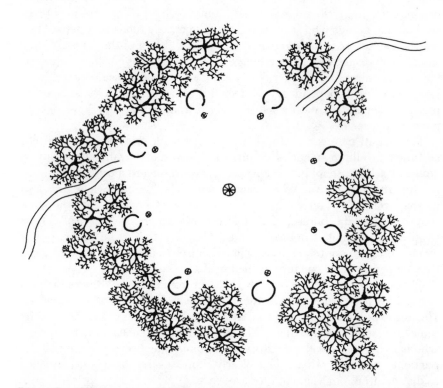

Figure 2   *Village structure of Mbuti in Zaire. Mbuti sociality is clearly manifested in the typically inward-facing nature of their hunting camps. Each household faces the center where a communal hearth, the symbol of their unity, is placed. Individual households have their own cooking hearths. However, because all members of a camp consider themselves a single "family," any individual can move freely from hearth to hearth. Sharing food merely reflects the sharing that the Mbuti work so hard for in maintaining an essentially social, cooperative, noncompetitive, and human culture. Illustration by Sally Bensusen.*

ognition of interdependency between humankind and the rest of the natural world is constantly repeated through life, and the child is taught true sociality through these symbols.

We teach our children other things, for example, through our "games." Stop and think what a game is and how totally contradictory it is to our professed values of equality. The essence of any game is that one starts equal. Yet the object is to compete and end up unequal. There are positive educational values in games in our society, but these games also make a virtue of inequality and sometimes of violence. They may be another step in the direction of dehumanization if we let them go uncontrolled. The Mbuti have what, superficially, resemble games but actually are merely pastimes. Giving just as much pleasure, these develop visual and other skills but are played in such a way that it is impossible to "win." There are no winners; there are no losers. This, actually, is the definition of a ritual, in which you start theoretically unequal and end up equal. So many Mbuti pastimes are, in fact, sacred rituals rather than secular games.

The Mbuti have developed hunting techniques that demand the closest, most intimate cooperation; competition is anathema. In the area where I worked, they hunted chiefly with nets. While setting up the nets they made jokes about each other: "Oh, I didn't see so-and-so, he looked like a tree." They are constantly referring to their proximity to the natural world. They recognize their ecological interdependence in very subtle ways, but they also make them overt. In the complex cooperation of the hunt, they are also working at the business of becoming social, of becoming fully human. Hunting involves killing, and many game wardens have told me—and I have seen it—that the hunters are the best conservers of all. Their own survival depends upon the hunt providing the right kind of cropping, but for the Mbuti there is no pleasure in killing.

The Mbuti have a legend that tells us this: "When God created the world, God created all living things immortal, and we did not kill. But one day, a Mbuti saw an antelope and killed it and ate it. And even though he ate all of it, so that it was all made use of, nonetheless he had killed and God was angry. Since that day, God has made all animals, including the four-legged animals, the two-legged animals, and all the others, mortal. So if only we can learn how to survive without killing we may regain our immortality." This is the kind of story these so-called "primitive" people tell. It shows in their enormous respect for life at the moment of the kill, when there is neither joy nor sorrow. Killing is something that has to be done, but they believe it is another step away from the immortality that might have been man's.

Being a natural part of the world for the Mbuti means being natural with themselves: the first menstrual period of a girl is celebrated with enormous joy. Why? Because it means that now she has the potential of becoming a mother. And what could be a greater occasion for joy for any girl than that? Everyone comes out to celebrate. Menstruation is considered a beautiful and natural thing and celebrated publicly and openly. They see nothing wrong with nature. Whatever it gives them, even death, they will accept.

They have a pastime—a hoop dance—to teach girls the kind of social relationship they are going to need to survive as human beings; not just to survive physically, but to survive as caring, loving, compassionate human beings in the forest. The girls celebrate menstruation by dancing together in and out of a small hoop in pairs. The hoop must not touch them, and they must not touch each other. During the dance, they sing together in parallel seconds, which is about the closest musical interval in which we can sing without falling into unison. In other words, they come close to being the same person, and yet each retains her own identity. The concept is that we are all individuals, and we are all different from each other, but let's get as close to each other as we possibly can.

These are a wise people, and they have survived. We have records, going back to the Fourth Dynasty in Egypt, that indicate the Mbuti were then a very similar people to what they are today. Here is a culture that clearly has survived thousands and thousands of years, and to have been like that then, the culture must have already existed for thousands of years. How old is our current modern industrial culture? A few hundred years. That is not very good proof of survivability. And I would say that cultures such as that of the Mbuti, which have survived as successfully as they have, have done so largely because of the proximity that individuals in the society see to the natural world around them, and the interdependence they feel with it and each other. And it is a world, above all, that they themselves perceive as being beautiful.

I should have learned about cultural extinction many years ago when I went to India as a young student to do some research in philosophy. I questioned why it is that human beings have this incredible facility for being unfaithful to their great and beautiful ideals. In reply, I was told the following story: The Supreme Being was, of course, all powerful. And in one of the many divine diversions he indulged in he created the earth, and it was beautiful, with mountains and valleys and oceans and rivers and deserts and plains. And he thought to himself that it was so beautiful that he would like to be a part of it. So the Supreme Being manifested himself on earth as a pig. Pigs are, if nothing else, in touch with the earth, and he found this was fun and good. He could grovel around in the dirt and that was delightful. Then he grew bored with being a pig all by himself. He was a male pig, so he divided himself and manifested another part of himself as a female pig. That was even more fun and gave him a lot more to do. Very shortly there were lots of little piglets. So the God Mother Pig and God Father Pig told the piglets, "Look, have a good time. This is our world. We made it. You are here to enjoy it. But remember, you really are gods. You are actually little godlets, not piglets." And the children said, "You mean anytime we want to we can be gods again?" The parents said, "Yes, certainly, anytime." And then the parents got tired of everything and died off. The piglets had more piglets, and they told the children, "You know, our parents told us that we were really gods and if we ever want to, we can be anything else we want." The young piglets said, "Well, what else is there to be? We are having such a good time, who'd want to be anything else?" And they went on groveling around in the dirt, filth, and muck, thinking that this was all there was to life. And when they had piglets they didn't even bother to tell their children what their idiotic old grandparents had said. That is why pigs think that they are pigs. And that is why, just as mistakenly, we think that we are whatever we think we are, and are just as easily convinced that our world is the best of all worlds.

I think that is a great story for, finally, it shows us how far we have already come from being what we were. And it shows us the danger that we face of ultimately becoming nothing more than a shadow of what we once were and thus a shadow of what we might have become.

References Cited and Additional Readings

Gennep, Arnold van
    1960.   *The Rites of Passage*. Chicago: University of Chicago Press.

Harako, R.
    1976.   The Mbuti as hunters: a study of ecological anthropology of the Mbuti Pygmies, 33–99. *Kyoto University African Studies*, Vol. X. (Kyoto, Japan).

Schebesta, P.
    1952.   *Les Pygmees du Congo Belge*. (Institut royal Colonial Belge.) Section des sciences morales et politiques. Memoirs, V. 26 (2), 432. (Bruxelles).

Southall, A., ed.
1961.   *Social Change in Modern Africa.* New York: Oxford University Press.

Turnbull, C.
1961.   *The Forest People.* New York: Simon and Schuster.

1962.   *The Lonely African.* New York: Simon and Schuster.

1972.   *The Ik, the Mountain People.* New York: Simon and Schuster.

1973.   *Africa and Change.* New York: Random House.

1976.   *Wayward Servants.* Westport: Greenwood Press.

1983.   *The Human Cycle.* New York: Simon and Schuster.